If These **WALLS** *Could* **TALK:**

SEATTLE SEAHAWKS

If These
WALLS
Could TALK:
SEATTLE SEAHAWKS

Stories from the
Seattle Seahawks Sideline,
Locker Room, and Press Box

Dave Wyman with Bob Condotta

30 YEARS®
TRIUMPH
B O O K S

Library of Congress Cataloging-in-Publication Data

Names: Wyman, Dave, author. | Condotta, Bob, author.
Title: If these walls could talk : Seattle Seahawks : stories from the
    Seattle Seahawks sideline, locker room, and press box / David Wyman with
    Bob Condotta.
Description: Chicago : Triumph Books LLC, 2019.
Identifiers: LCCN 2019018162 | ISBN 9781629376967
Subjects: LCSH: Seattle Seahawks (Football team)—History. | Seattle
    Seahawks (Football team)—Anecdotes. | Football players—United
    States—Anecdotes. | Football—United States—History.
Classification: LCC GV956.S4 .W95 2019 | DDC 796.332/6409797772—dc23
LC record available at https://lccn.loc.gov/2019018162

This book is available in quantity at special discounts for your group or organization. For further information, contact:
    Triumph Books LLC
    814 North Franklin Street
    Chicago, Illinois 60610
    (312) 337-0747
    www.triumphbooks.com

Printed in U.S.A.
ISBN: 978-1-62937-696-7
Design by Nord Compo
Photos courtesy of AP Images

To my wife, Shannen, for putting up with me
burying myself in my computer to write this book,
and to my children, Jake and Kendall, for telling me
when something was "boring and sucks."

—*DW*

To my sons, Curtis and Marcus,
who have made this all worth it.

—*BC*

CONTENTS

FOREWORD

As the door closed on the tiny puddle jumper of my first ever airplane flight, I was in fear. Not only was I in the air and climbing, but there was more unknown ahead. I was heading to my first minicamp with the Seattle Seahawks. I was a wide-eyed kid about to fulfill a dream I had since I was 5 and growing up in Wisconsin, visualizing maybe someday playing for Vince Lombardi and the Green Bay Packers. It was May 15, 1980, a date easy to remember because Mount St. Helens erupted three days later. As I think back, it's strange that I got to see a mountain erupt and then the Kingdome implode 20 years later.

The Seahawks were still a young franchise then, playing their first game in 1976. What I mostly knew of the Seahawks were their special teams orchestrated by the guru himself, assistant coach Rusty Tillman, and kicker Efren Herrera, who may be the best receiving kicker in the history of the NFL. Things slowly would change, though, and for a while in the mid-1980s, the Seahawks rose to national prominence, setting the foundation for what is now one of the best franchises in all of sports.

And in a few years, we'd be in the playoffs one game away from the Super Bowl. Who could have imagined that? That's what I call visualizing! But I could not have visualized Dave Wyman writing a book. In all seriousness, Dave has an absolute love for the game. And after playing in the NFL in the 1980s and 1990s, he now sits aside the legend himself, Steve Raible, doing color commentary on the radio broadcasts for the Seahawks. I can't think of any better pairing. Both of these guys are passionate ambassadors for the city of Seattle, the state of Washington, and the Northwest.

Dave and I might disagree at times; he is ultracompetitive in that department, too. But overall I'd like to think we had the same destination in mind. It's just how we got there that might have been different at times. Dave showed his courage and guts long before he got to the NFL. He suffered a gruesome knee injury his senior year at Stanford. Someone on the sideline that day told me he'd never seen a leg bend back like that.

He was then drafted by the Seahawks in the second round in 1987. Imagine coming off major ACL, MCL, and patella tendon surgery and straight into an expectation-laden business.

But he persevered and became a great player, a better teammate, and a close friend. Heck, I even let him babysit my boys when they were infants. I, however, did hear of one incident when my son, Mikey, bit Dave on the stomach while wrestling with him.

Dave can have biting commentary, too. As you'll see in this book, he isn't one to mince words. This book offers great insight into the inner workings of the Seahawks' front office, particularly in the last decade, as Pete Carroll and John Schneider have built the team into one of the most successful in the NFL and brought Seattle its first Super Bowl title.

He goes into vivid detail about the excitement of being drafted, the physical pain he endured, and the agonizing realization when it was finally over. He gives you a look into the linebackers' perspective. He brings you right into the trenches, and you will get to know the current and former players and personalities on and off the field.

That brings me back to the start of my Seahawks career. I was in Minneapolis for the connection to Seattle and started to walk onto the plane, and there was this mountain of a man in front of me. It was 6'6" and 270 pounds of Ron Essink, or Shank, as he was affectionately called. As we got situated into our first-class seats—another first for me—I found out the offensive tackle was a 10th-round pick. Shank would go on to protect my blind side as our left tackle through the glory days of the early '80s, and we became best friends. An All-American in both football and wrestling at Grand Valley State, he was a workout fiend. Being in peak shape was the standard for him.

My first impression of Seattle was one word: beautiful. You could see the mountains, the water, the blue skies with clouds floating. It was like that old TV show, *Here Come the Brides*.

We got off the plane and were shuttled to the Bellevue Holiday Inn. Maybe that doesn't sound like much, but for me—coming from tiny Milton College—it was the nicest place.

Our first practice was Friday, May 15, and there were two rookies to a locker. We were told to bring our helmets and shoes. Our Milton College helmets were gold like Notre Dame's, and my shoes were rubber-bottomed Riddells with the cleats worn down like a bowling shoe. Practicing on the best manicured football fields and seeing sparkling Lake Washington was sure something.

The next day I got called up from the field to the general manager's office. I went upstairs with my helmet and cleats still on, thinking I was getting cut. I didn't have an agent, but they offered me a three-year contract with an option plus a signing bonus of $500. It must have been the quickest negotiation ever. I walked out of there on cloud nine.

Football was the ultimate opportunity for me. Growing up in central Wisconsin, the life options there were basically working at a paper mill or a dairy farm like the one my dad, Myron Krieg, grew up on. Eventually, my dad got a job with the Wisconsin State Patrol. The only sport my dad played was farm league baseball. Milking cows, bailing hay, and shoveling manure were jobs that had to be done every day at 5:00 AM and 5:00 PM. That work ethic shown by Grandpa and my family would become invaluable to me. After my senior year of high school, my dad suggested college. I was a good athlete, but I wasn't All-Conference or anything like that, so I had no offers.

My high school coach, Dick Ambrosino, recommended Milton, a school that had 300 students at the time and was located in the southern part of Wisconsin in a town that had a population of about 3,000. Head coach Rudy Gaddini told me I'd have a shot at quarterback. We were seven deep at that spot, and I had to start at the bottom. I had an inauspicious start at Milton, separating my shoulder in my first scrimmage game. After five weeks of healing and with the offense struggling, Coach Gaddini put me in. If the beginning was a little rocky, I quickly found out that Milton was an unbelievably fortuitous place for me. I was able to play four years, getting invaluable experience and reps. We did not have reporters in the locker room or TV coverage. In a small way it bonded us as teammates because not one person was getting the blame or credit. I'd learn later that I wished I had more reps with reporters.

But after four years at Milton in the rearview mirror and a signed contract with the Seahawks, it was go time. My next flight was to Spokane to start training camp in Cheney at Eastern Washington University. It was evident immediately that this experience was more intense than any game I'd ever been in, and it was only practice! This was back in the day when teams brought in seven quarterbacks. A couple of the quarterbacks got homesick, and another was cut. After a matter of weeks, I was all the way up to fourth string.

That first camp when Jack Patera was still the coach was far and away the most tortuous camp I remember. The mental grind for any player is difficult, but for a quarterback, it's even more. You are expected to simply say the play while at same time, thinking, *Which way do I turn? Who do I throw to? What's going to be the coverage? What's the snap count?*

It's one thing that always impressed me about Russell Wilson when the Seahawks brought him in. He was so ready and so prepared, and Carroll and Schneider were so smart to draft him. During his rookie year, he played a preseason game against the Kansas City Chiefs. Matt Flynn, a veteran brought in to be the No. 1 quarterback, was unable to play due to a sore elbow so Wilson got the start. I watched as he just took control of the game from the start, and if it got crazy, he'd scramble the way he still does today. He was poised, looking downfield to not just make a play, but also come up with the right play time and again. Having learned a lot about the quarterback position through the years, I can say there are just not many like Wilson. He's a winner, a man with integrity. I so enjoy watching him play.

But things didn't go as smoothly for me right out of the gate as they did for Wilson. I'd never even seen or been in a dome before my first game. My uniform was in my locker, and it had my name on the back. Believe it or not, that was the first time I'd ever had my name on a jersey. My folks were able to fly out to watch me play the fourth quarter.

There weren't many in the crowd for pregame warmups. Throwing inside was effortless; there was no wind, rain, or snow. It was ideal for a quarterback to come out for the start of a game. But as kickoff neared, the place was packed, and claustrophobia set in. It became noisy, and I started to hyperventilate. I was hunched over in the nearest end zone. Watching the speed of the players and the hits was amazing. You don't realize what it's like until you're right there in the middle of it. The hits were like a prizefight.

With all the anxiety and trepidation weighing on me, I ran onto the field. I tried to remember the simple play given to me—*I Right 42.* The rest of the guys broke the huddle, and I stood alone, watching the offensive line run to the line of scrimmage. I barked out the signals (a color and numbers), got the snap, turned, and handed off to Tony Benjamin. My first play was over, and I suddenly felt both relief and pride, even though it was just a handoff. But as a rookie, everything you do is momentous, critiqued, and tests your intestinal fortitude. By the end of my first preseason, I'd done enough to make the team. I called my dad telling him I had made it. He was proud but pragmatic, reminding me to continue working as hard as I did to get this opportunity.

And I did. Every practice I was out there trying to prove I belonged. I loved practice.

It was an amazing feat just to get that far, considering the longest of odds an undrafted quarterback from Milton had to make an NFL roster. The next offseason prior to the 1981 season, Jerry Rhome, my first quarterback coach, had a quarterback school for two months. This is when I studied more intensely than ever. The results were slow; the first few weeks my grades were in the 60s. The veterans—Jim Zorn, Sam Adkins, Steve Meyer (who hurt his neck my rookie year, opening up a roster spot for me)—all knew this stuff. The razzing I received from those guys was humbling and incentivizing. After a month I was getting 80s and an occasional 90. Once I understood the mental terminology and was able to identify the defenses, the game slowed down for me.

During that second year, I was getting some mop-up assignments. When Zorn hurt his ankle in the 13th game, I got my first start against the New York Jets and their famed New York Sack Exchange defense led by Mark Gastineau and Joe Klecko. Amazingly, we beat them 27–23. My first pass was a touchdown on a slant to Sam McCullum. It was a surreal feeling. We played great defense, and our offensive line kept that great defense at bay.

For all of this, I'd like to thank the original owners, Elmer and Kitty Nordstrom. I'd never heard of the Nordstrom store before becoming a Seahawks player, but they turned out to be great owners and the nicest folks. I will forever remember the look on Mr. Nordstrom's face after we beat the Miami Dolphins in the playoffs on New Year's Eve of 1983. No one had expected us to win, as we were 14-point underdogs. Elmer was inside the small visitors' locker room. His franchise had just beaten the vaunted Dolphins with their Killer Bees defense, an offense led by a rookie named Dan Marino, and a squad coached by the legendary Don Shula. Elmer acted like a proud parent, affectionately going around to congratulate all the players. It was a team effort and quite an atmosphere.

We headed to the AFC Championship Game, and the Seahawks franchise was on the map. It ended a week later in a loss to the Los Angeles Raiders, a team we had beaten twice that year, but that Raiders team was a veteran group that had won the Super Bowl a couple of years prior. Our youth at quarterback and all over hurt us, as the game seemed too big for us at that time. I certainly needed to improve. But the Seahawks would get there again in 2006 with Matt Hasselbeck and then again a few years later with Wilson. Turn the page now and join my friend, Dave Wyman, to read about how it all unfolded.

—*Dave Krieg*
Seahawks quarterback 1980–1991

INTRODUCTION

That I would one day end up in the position I am today—the color analyst for the radio broadcasts of one of the most successful NFL teams in the league following a nine-year NFL playing career—is the kind of life I could hardly have even dreamed of as a kid.

My brother, Mike, and I grew up in small logging towns in Northern California and often spent Sunday afternoons watching NFL games on TV and thinking how great it would be to one day be one of these players. It seemed a world away back then. But once we started playing high school football in Reno, Nevada, Mike got some attention from college scouts. And two years later, I did, too. I was fortunate enough to follow my big brother to Stanford to play college football.

My freshman year at Stanford included games like beating the No. 1-ranked Washington Huskies, watching John Elway bring us back time and time again, and being on the kickoff team on "The Play" in the Big Game in 1982. Before that rivalry game, I was told that if we defeated Cal, we would not only go to the Peach Bowl, but I also would be the starter in a college bowl game. Four or five laterals later, our season was over, and we wouldn't reach a bowl game until my redshirt fifth year. I grew up watching college bowl games on television and thought playing in a game like that would be the best thing I ever did in my life. So you understand why the video of that play still makes me angry.

To say it was a rocky road to get to that point is an understatement. My junior year of 1984 I was chop blocked by Arizona wide receiver Vance Johnson, who I actually would later play with on the Denver Broncos. The block dislocated my right knee, leaving me with no detectable pulse in my lower right leg. I was in jeopardy of an amputation for about 30 minutes. Eventually, they found my pulse, but I had torn nearly every ligament and tendon on the lateral side of my knee. It took until the spring of 1986 to get back on the field.

Fortunately, I made it back basically as good as new. After my senior year, I was named *The Sporting News* All-American and All-Pac-10. After we played in the 1986 Gator Bowl, the push to get into the pros began. I had an interesting conversation with my communications department mentor about my prospects in the NFL. I explained to him that I needed to take two weeks off: one week to play in the East/West Shrine Game and another to prepare for and attend the Scouting Combine in Indianapolis. He said to me: "How important is this? You're going to miss a lot of time. How many players from Stanford even make it into the NFL?" At this time Stanford was not the football factory that it is now.

I told him that I was slated to be selected in the first two rounds of the draft. He responded, "Well you've got to concentrate on your major. How much money can you make playing football anyway?"

I said, "Well, somewhere between $175,000 and $250,000 a year." His eyes widened, and his advice was, "Oh you should definitely go! Take all the time you need." It was sound advice, and that same mentor helped me get my degree in communications. On draft day my family and I huddled up in my brother's condo in Reno because he was one of the few people who had this little channel called ESPN on his cable package.

The draft started early, so we all slept on the floor in front of his television. By about 10:00 AM, I got a call from the Seattle Seahawks, and they made me the 45th pick in the 1987 NFL Draft. As they say, the rest is history.

I've spent much of the rest of the last 30 years associated with the Seahawks—first as a player and then doing radio and TV work in Seattle. The 2018 season was my first working the entire regular season alongside the legendary Steve Raible on the Seahawks' gameday broadcasts. This book reviews many of the highlights of my career with the Seahawks, as well as what has happened to the Seahawks since then—from the Chuck Knox and Kingdome days, to the team's first Super Bowl run under Mike Holmgren, and then all the ups and downs (mostly ups) of the Pete Carroll era.

Due to my media roles, I've had a front-row seat to all the great Seahawks moments—and a few we might like back—that have happened since Carroll became the coach in 2010, setting off the greatest run in team history. I was there when Marshawn Lynch ripped off a run that gave new meaning to the term "Beast Mode" and caused an earthquake in Seattle. I was there when a little-known quarterback—known mostly by many for being little—named Russell Wilson began to wow everyone in the summer and fall of 2012. I was there when Richard Sherman's tip sent the Seahawks back to the Super Bowl. And I was there when Seattle completed the job two weeks later in New Jersey. In the pages that follow, I'll tell you a little about myself and a lot more about the Seahawks and what always has been an entertaining NFL ride.

CHAPTER 1
PLAYING WITH "THE BOZ"

The morning of my graduation from Stanford University, I unfolded the Sporting Green—the sports page in the *San Francisco Chronicle*—and read the page two headline: "Seahawks Get Bosworth In Supplemental Draft." Two months prior I had been drafted by the Seattle Seahawks in the second round to replace an aging linebacker named Keith Butler and play alongside phenomenal special teams player Fredd Young, who had emerged as a defensive talent as well.

I had scraped and crawled my way back from one of the worst knee injuries in college football history two years prior. I had a total knee dislocation that left me temporarily in risk of losing my right leg and perpetually concerned that my knee wouldn't hold up enough to even allow me to walk without a limp. My hard work, though, was rewarded with a senior season that included being named to *The Sporting News* All-American team and All-Pac-10 honors at linebacker in 1986.

That season my nemesis was Brian Bosworth. With no Internet in the 1980s, legend and word of mouth was how you heard about other players, and any linebacker that was mentioned in the news had to be a phenom. He was the next Dick Butkus and the be-all/end-all linebacker of all time. And he was going to be my teammate and probably push me out of the picture in Seattle.

While I arrived in Seattle with little fanfare, "The Boz" arrived in a helicopter. I had a bad haircut and Levi's; The Boz had an iconic mohawk and looked like he had just walked off the set of *Miami Vice*. Bosworth drove a white convertible Corvette, and I drove a 1982 Chevy S-10 pickup truck. To add insult to injury, they made him my roommate during camp. But what I found was that Bosworth was a good friend and teammate. The Boz, however, was another story. Bosworth would give you a ride to the airport; The Boz would tell you to take a cab. Bosworth was a great neighbor; The Boz treated you like you were part of his service staff.

But two things have been forgotten. No matter what Bosworth says now about the alter ego called The Boz and how it ruined his life, we had a lot of fun with him being The Boz. We never waited in line. We once went grocery shopping while drinking beers off the shelf, and no one even noticed because they were so in awe of him. We always got the best treatment, no matter where we went. It was perfect for me because I loved playing pro football and was happy in my anonymity.

And secondly in Bosworth's rookie season in 1987, he was most decidedly not a bust. He played his tail off. In a strike-shortened year, he had four sacks, including one that left Kansas City Chiefs quarterback Bill Kenney with a bloody face. He recovered two fumbles, one of which came up just one yard shy of a touchdown. He made plays all over the field. And yet two plays against the Los Angeles Raiders are all that anyone remembers: a Bo Jackson run down the sidelines in a *Monday Night Football* game (the run in which Jackson also outran future Hall of Famer Kenny Easley "on his way to Tacoma," as Al Michaels so famously put it) and a goal-line play in which Bosworth simply did not get his head across the front of Jackson. Neither was anything close to being embarrassing for even the best linebacker in the league. But The Boz had built an image of invincibility, and as well as the rookie linebacker played that year, Jackson single-handedly shattered that image.

After that game Seattle fans turned a little bit on The Boz. Seattle is different. This isn't Los Angeles or New York City. People in Seattle are more down to earth. They won't have the wool pulled over their eyes, and it seemed to me that people felt fleeced by The Boz—like they were sold a bill of goods. I started alongside Bosworth in 1988 and, as I started to make plays and he played less and less, I felt like Seattle fans rewarded me for being a soft-spoken, underdog player. When Bosworth and I would go out in town, people would come up and say hello to both of us, but every once in a while, fans would stick it to The Boz by shaking my hand and ignoring him. But that was Seattle for you.

Bosworth was the Vince McMahon of football. It's such a team sport that no one had ever thought to be self-promoting. The Boz would sell whether you loved him or hated him, and it was pretty brilliant actually, and there was no better example of that than in Denver in 1987.

The offensive line on any team sticks together and they collectively decided that they didn't like The Boz. I always say that offensive linemen are an understated group who are bonded together by misery. That's because no one ever mentions an offensive lineman unless they screw up. It was my impression that the o-line as a group tended to regulate morality on the team as well. In Denver they found out that there were "Boz Buster" T-shirts for sale at the Broncos' Mile High Stadium in anticipation for the arrival of The Boz. So they went into the stands in Denver and bought Boz Buster T-shirts before the game started. They put them on and proudly paraded past Boz's locker while wearing the T-shirt that had his likeness on it with a big red slash through it. I was sitting next to Bosworth, and he took it surprisingly well. He chuckled and said, "I think I'll buy new seat covers for my Corvette with the money those guys just spent on my T-shirts." Bosworth's company, 44 Blues, had made the T-shirts and marketed them in every NFL stadium the Seahawks were headed to that year. What a brilliant move!

I must admit that Bosworth was much more streetwise than I was. It did me some good to hang around with The Boz. I was still that little kid that was just happy to be playing pro football, and Bosworth had what was probably the appropriate amount of cynicism.

My first start in the NFL was the next year's game in Denver. It was the opener in 1988. I was so nervous that all I could get down in the pregame meal was a bowl of Froot Loops. But I puked that version of the breakfast of champions into a garbage can on the way onto the field. I played well in a tough game, in which two players had to be carted off the field. Broncos safety Mike Harden laid a brutal hit on wide receiver Steve Largent (that would be paid back later in the season), and I was involved in a collision that left me dazed and bloody and another player temporarily paralyzed. During that latter play, one of the first few in the game, the Broncos lined up tight end Clarence Kay in the backfield as a fullback. He led the way on an iso blast, and he and I collided in the backfield. His helmet hit me square in the chin, leaving me dazed, but I was just conscious enough to fall on a Tony Dorsett fumble that nose guard Joe Nash caused in the backfield. As I sat on the sideline getting my chin stapled shut, I said to the trainer,

"That guy knocked the shit out of me!" He replied, "Well, you got the better of that hit." I looked onto the field to see Kay being loaded onto a stretcher and carried off the field. I can't say that I felt bad about it, but I was relieved to see him standing on the sidelines in street clothes later in the game. My first start was a win, and I felt like I had a hand in the victory.

Going into my rookie year, my agent Marvin Demoff told me, "Your rookie year is going to be tough. So if you spend any money at all, spend it on a decent apartment, a nice comfortable couch, and a big TV." Demoff was always right, and my rookie year was indeed tough. Training camp seemed interminable, and an old shoulder injury from college kept popping up, making things even worse. I regularly got my butt kicked in practice, and the coaches seemed disappointed in my play. And then just to make everything even more terrible, we went on strike.

This was the 1987 season and also the second strike in the game in six seasons. Much of 1982 had been wiped out. This one didn't last as long—just three games and another week of work lost. From what I knew, I was not on board with going on strike. But once again, my wise agent told me to go along with my teammates because I was going to be with them a long time.

When that was resolved—leaving me with four fewer game checks— my agent and I decided that I should ask for a trade.

It was clear that the Seahawks were happy with Bosworth as their linebacker of the future. Demoff told me to march into Chuck Knox's office and ask to be traded to the San Francisco 49ers. Now Demoff had greased the skids for this trade, but the thought of me demanding something from the most intimidating man I'd ever met did not sit well with me. But I did it, and the trade happened. When I left Seattle, there was an article about my departure on page three of *The Seattle Times*. When I got to San Francisco, which was just 45 minutes from Stanford, my name was on the front page of the *San Francisco Chronicle*'s Sporting Green.

Fellow Seahawks linebacker Brian Bosworth watches from the sideline during his rookie season in 198?.

"49ers Get Dave Wyman" was the headline.

You may not remember me as a 49er, even though I had a jersey. I was No. 59. I put that on and started to trot out to my first practice with my new 49ers helmet, but someone stopped me and said, "There is a problem with your physical." Thirty-six hours later, I was on a plane back to Seattle. That shoulder problem that I mentioned in camp was a concern for the doctors in San Francisco. The way I understood it was that the 49ers asked that the trade deal be sweetened on their side if I did not react well to the shoulder surgery I needed. Apparently, Seattle general manager Mike McCormack, who wasn't on board with the trade in the first place, responded: "Just send him back."

That's the NFL for you. The 49ers felt that I needed surgery, but I flew back to Seattle and was running down, covering kickoffs the next Sunday. I did have offseason surgery on my shoulder and by the end of the 1988 training camp I had won the starting linebacker job next to Bosworth. A brutal rookie year paid off, and I felt like I was back to being a football player again. Everything slowed down for me, and I was the player I was in high school and college.

My rookie year in 1987 was a bizarre experience for me with the strike, the failed trade, and the disappointing 9–6 record. The Seahawks were picked by more than a few analysts, including those in *Sports Illustrated*, to go to the Super Bowl that year after having finished 10–6 the previous season and then adding The Boz. An *SI* story the week the season began had the headline: "Steve Largent and the rest of the Seahawks figure to meet a Giant obstacle in Super Bowl XXII." Paul Zimmerman wrote: "The Vikings loom as the NFL's most intriguing dark horse, a distinction Seattle would enjoy except that everyone is jumping on the Seahawks' bandwagon."

But we didn't quite make it. We didn't even win the division. That honor went to Denver. Instead, we had to settle for a wild-card bid and lost to the Houston Oilers in the playoffs. It was a welcome-to-the-NFL, kid type of season. But my second year in 1988 was fun for me, and it felt less like a business and more like a game. We won the AFC West with a 9–7 record and made the playoffs. That year ended with a disappointing loss in the wild-card round to the eventual AFC champion Cincinnati Bengals.

CHAPTER 2
MY FAVORITE
TEAMMATES

I played for the Seahawks from 1987 to 1992 before finishing my career with the Denver Broncos. While on the Seahawks, we won the franchise's first division title, taking the AFC West with a win against the Raiders in Los Angeles in the final game of the 1988 regular season.

I was also a part of the worst season in Seahawks history—a 2–14 record in 1992—though the less said about that, the better. As much as the season records and the games, what stands out years later are the people I met along the way. Here are some of my favorite teammates and coaches from my time playing with the Seahawks.

Steve Largent

Largent's nickname was "Yoda" for obvious reasons. He was small, wise, and a master of the game of football. Amongst Steve's habits, he was always reading self-improvement books. I used to think to myself: *He should be writing self-improvement books.* He would play out an entire football game on the practice field before every game on either Friday or Saturday.

After our walk-through was over and everyone was heading into the locker room to shower, he would remain on the field all by himself. He would crouch down with his hands on his knees as if he were in a real huddle, clap his hands to break the huddle, jog out to his position, simulate a pass route or a blocking assignment, jog back to the huddle, and repeat. I had never seen it before.

He would consult any coach who could help him improve as a player. I once saw him having a conversation with defensive line coach George Dyer about how he teaches his players to get blockers' hands off of them.

Largent was also part of any Seahawks fan's favorite moments when he got the ultimate payback on Denver Broncos safety Mike Harden. Our 1988 opener was in Denver, and it was a hard-hitting slugfest that ended in a 21–14 Seahawks win. Near the end of the game, Largent caught a pass over the middle of the field, and Harden dislocated him from the ball with a forearm to the face. Largent was knocked out temporarily, and it took him several minutes to get off the field.

Fast forward 14 weeks when the Broncos came to town, and that same player, Harden, picked off a pass, and during the run back, Largent returned the favor with a brutal, yet legal hit. He hit Harden so hard that he dislodged him from the ball. If that wasn't enough, he also recovered the fumble. It was revenge, something I'm sure Largent would normally disapprove of. But it was done in the right way and within the rules of the game. It was *so* Largent!

I could probably have outrun Largent as could every single corner-back or safety that Largent played against. Covering him or keeping him from catching the ball was a totally different story. There's a great picture at Seahawks headquarters of Largent catching a touchdown pass. The defender is turned around and facing the wrong way. It's kind of like when you put your T-shirt on backward and inside out. That's what he would do to defensive backs. Largent retired after the 1989 season while holding most NFL receiving records. His No. 80 was immediately retired, but it remains a constant presence in the stands at CenturyLink Field every Sunday.

Cortez Kennedy

He went wherever he wanted to go. Kennedy was not built like Tarzan. I'm not sure if he was particularly strong in the weight room. On the field, though, he could move 600-pound double teams, knife through or around any blocker, and always get to the quarterback. I played off of him the way a pilot fish swims around a shark, picking up tackles and fumbles caused by Kennedy's destruction.

I was responsible for slanting him toward the play based on what our defensive coordinator Tom Catlin saw in certain formations. But Tez liked to go to his left. I would try to slant him right sometimes, and he would shake me off like a pitcher does to a catcher calling pitches. Once on the sidelines, Catlin asked me, "Why did you slant them left?" I said, "Because Tez wanted to go left." Catlin responded, "Good idea."

Wide receiver Steve Largent catches a pass in 1985, when he led the NFL with 1,287 receiving yards.

Kennedy was the only player I ever knew that actually loved training camp. In the 1980s and '90s, the two-a-days of training camp were a grind. I once went through five straight two-a-day, full-pad, full-contact practices. You would see guys dragging themselves down the hallways of the dorms and into bed. But not Tez. He was joyful and happy and always playing pranks on his teammates. One night at about 2:00 AM, I awoke to go to the bathroom. I left my door open and barely opened my eyes the entire way there and back. As I settled back into bed, Tez jumped out of my closet like a jack-in-the-box and scared the hell out of me. He made sure everyone on the team heard that story the next day.

Kennedy passed away in his sleep in May of 2017 at the way-too-young age of 48. I miss him every day.

Tom Catlin

Our defensive coordinator was so good that he was named as the best assistant in the NFL in 1992, even though we went 2–14. We lost nine games that year in which our offense scored seven points or less. Our offense scored only 140 points that year, the fewest of any team in NFL history in a 16-game season. I spent six years with Catlin, and he was the best coach I ever had.

Catlin was the kind of coach that veterans respected, and the older I got, the more I appreciated him. He was dry as the desert and all business. I was friends with my coaches at Stanford, and they cared about my life off the field. Catlin didn't seem to care about anything but coaching defense. But as I developed into a pro, mostly because of Catlin, I came to appreciate his businesslike approach. Once you were a veteran, Catlin would reward you by asking about your life off the field.

Catlin's forte was installing a defense. He always said, "Save your questions to the end." There were never questions when Catlin was done. One of my proudest moments in the NFL was when I asked a question at the end of a defensive install, and Catlin replied, "Good question."

Another proud moment was when I actually made him laugh. It looked like his face would crack.

Catlin was a linebacker at Oklahoma and then with the Cleveland Browns. We played a game in Cleveland in 1988, and I remember watching Catlin gaze around the field and up into the stands. It was like he was transporting himself back to 1953 when men wore ties and hats to the games. That ol' linebacker attitude came out when the Seahawks played the AFC Championship Game in 1984, and this story made me like him even more. After an improbable road win against the Miami Dolphins, Seattle was one game away from the Super Bowl and in Los Angeles facing the Raiders. After the Seahawks loss, a raucous Raiders fanbase stormed the field, and it was a mess. There were too few security people and too many rabid fans. Catlin decided to circle the wagons—or linebackers, as was the case—and get off the field quickly. The team was nearly to the tunnel when a particularly obnoxious fan broke through their group and wagged a finger in Catlin's face and cursed him. In one motion Catlin slammed him against the tunnel wall with one hand and dropped him with a single punch with the other. He then turned to linebacker Sam Merriman and in his dry manner said, "I hope that wasn't a friend of yours."

Chuck Knox

Coach Knox taught me to be a pro. He was not very personable and very businesslike, but I came to really appreciate that about him. I used to call him the "Mona Lisa" because—no matter where you stood at practice—it seemed like he was looking right at you. He had his famous phrases, which I call Knoxisms.

> "Don't tell me how rough the water is; bring the boat in."
> "Nobody wants to hear your sad story. Working will, wishing won't."
> "Don't piss in my face and tell me it's raining. Nobody wants to hear your sad story."
> "Play the hand you're dealt."

On the way back from the airport after a long trip back east, our bus driver got lost driving to the facility in Kirkland. Before long, players started complaining, and the driver started making excuses. This prompted Steve Largent to shout out "Don't tell me how rough the road is; just bring the bus in." Then others chimed in, saying, "No one wants to hear your sad story."

I was in a slump in 1991 and not playing my best football. Knox came up to me and told me, "If you don't start playing better, you're going to be standing on the sidelines next to me." He was direct, matter of fact, and terrifying. But they say professionals want to be told the truth, and as bad as that felt, I appreciated it.

In 1990 we beat the Kansas City Chiefs, our division foe, in Kansas City, and it was something we had not done since 1980. Kansas City was one of the few airports where you had to walk through the airport like a normal traveler. We won on the last play of the game, and everybody was in a celebratory mood, to say the least. On the way to the plane, a few players trickled into a tiny airport bar near the gate. Then a few more went in to have a quick pop before the flight and to celebrate. Pretty soon nearly the entire team was jammed into this little bar. I remember seeing travelers on the way to their flights, peering into a small bar filled with extremely large human beings. We all sort of lost track of time, and suddenly Knox, who had been on the plane, strolled into the bar with a stern look on his face. The room, as was always the case when Knox walked in, went dead silent. Then Knox reached into his pocket and pulled out a couple of $100 bills and slapped them down on the bar and announced that the flight would be delayed.

Similarly, we beat the Los Angeles Raiders in the hellhole that was the Los Angeles Memorial Coliseum in those days. The buses pulled out about four blocks from the stadium. Bus No. 1, Knox's bus, pulled up to a liquor store. Knox sent two defensive linemen into the store with a wad of cash. Five minutes later both players each carried about six cases of beer out of the liquor store. It was a fun ride home.

Dave Krieg

Krieg was the most competitive teammate I ever had. Whether it was cribbage in the training room, booray on the team plane, or on the sidelines of a game while we were down three touchdowns, Krieg always thought he could win. One example is from that 1990 game at Kansas City, which led to our airport bar celebration. We had not won there throughout the entire 1980s except for in 1980. It was a weird deal because we usually beat the Chiefs at the Kingdome, but they would hammer us at Arrowhead Stadium. In 1984 the Seahawks beat the Chiefs 45–0 at home and then lost to them 34–7 in Kansas City.

Anyway, Krieg had been sacked seven times that day by Hall of Fame pass rusher Derrick Thomas, and it seemed we were about to lose to them again. But on a play that ended with no time left on the clock, Krieg ducked out of what would've been Thomas' eighth sack of Krieg and threw a fastball to Paul Skansi for the winning touchdown. You would think that Krieg might have surrendered at that point. After getting sacked seven times by the same guy, you would think your psyche would have a tendency to get worn down. That kind of thing didn't happen to Krieg. He spun out of that sack, ran back to his left, and threw the ball across his body to his right. The frozen rope nearly knocked Skansi down and led to our win.

Krieg was from tiny Milton College in Wisconsin and, of course, a free agent when he came into the league. He told me that there is no Milton College anymore. I said, "You mean the football program?" He replied, "No there's no Milton College anymore." I used to kid him that they turned Milton College into a Chuck E. Cheese. That made his story even more improbable, and it's exactly how you would describe his career. Krieg enjoyed a 19-year NFL career, and I think he's Hall of Fame material. Going into the 2019 season, he's 23rd in NFL history with 38,147 yards, ahead of the likes of Jim Kelly, Steve Young, Troy Aikman, and Kurt Warner. He's even higher in touchdowns (in 18th place with 261 of them) and ahead of guys like Dan Fouts and

Terry Bradshaw. I know the argument might be that he didn't go to a Super Bowl like a lot of those guys did. But Krieg played with a lot of teams (six in all) and had just two losing seasons in 14 years as his team's primary starting quarterback.

Jacob Green

Green is one of nine players who is enshrined in the Seahawks' Ring of Honor. Of those players, he may be the one that fans today know the least about, but he should not be forgotten.

He's still the player by which any other Seahawks pass rusher has to be judged. Consider that he still holds the franchise record with 97.5 sacks. That's 24 more than any other player, making that a record that may take a really long time for someone to break. He also had 16 in a season, which remains second in team history, and four in a game, which remains tied for a team record. He also was voted a defensive team captain four straight years, a stretch that coincided with four of my first years.

He helped me become a pro. Tough but fair, he was the player version of Chuck Knox. I remember how good it felt when Green accepted me as a professional and an equal. There's a reason that Green is still a part of the Seahawks organization. (Green and Steve Largent are the two players on the team's group of official ambassadors, an organization set up in 2009 to advise the team's ownership on any issue relating to the franchise.)

We were on a losing streak one year, and Green kicked the coaches out of a team meeting and stood up in the front of the room and said: "Who is gonna make a play? I'm gonna get three sacks!" He went out and got three sacks that day. I never doubted him again.

Rufus Porter

"Ruuuuuff" is a chant that you would hear in the Kingdome in the late 1980s and early 1990s. Porter had made the team as a free agent in

1988 out of Southern University, which was not exactly a football powerhouse. He made the team and his name by covering kickoffs. Porter was famous for his "flying 40," which was something the great Rusty Tillman, a special teams coach, had used to measure a player's speed covering a kickoff. Back in the days when you could get a 10-yard run up to the kickoff line, Tillman would record your 40 time from the line where the ball was kicked to 40 yards downfield *with* the benefit of the 10-yard head start. There was no one faster, and Porter made tackle after tackle covering kicks. My first memory of that was a kickoff in a game that went to the opponents' goal line. By the time the returner had gotten to the 5-yard line, Porter had re-directed him into another player for a tackle on the 8-yard line.

Later in his career, he developed into a great pass rusher. Just as he was covering kicks, Porter was relentless when rushing the quarterback. He also had a unique ability to turn the corner or rush the edge of an offensive tackle, going full speed while leaning at a 45-degree angle. He was a great teammate off the field. He was always happy and good for a laugh. Porter was what some guys would call "country." It's not a bad thing. It just means that he's from a small town and kind of naïve to the ways of the world; that's what was charming about him. He was *not* charming to opposing quarterbacks. During his seven seasons as a Seahawks player, he compiled 37.5 sacks.

Joe Nash

When I think of Nash, the term "workhorse" comes to mind. He was listed at 6' 3" 280, but that was being generous. That only means that what he did on the field was that much more impressive. He played his entire 15-year career with the Seahawks and compiled 47.5 sacks, which is hard to do as a nose guard in a 3-4 defense, and almost 800 tackles in 218 games. He also had a knack for blocking kicks. In spite of his lack of height, he is tied with Craig Terrill with eight blocks in his career and had three blocks in one season. Both are Seahawks records.

Nash was an All-Pro and Pro Bowler in 1984 and really performed well his entire career, but he was a guy who thought he was going to get cut every year. From the time I played with him in 1987 until 1992, they were always trying to replace Nash with someone faster or bigger or younger, but by the end of training camp, it was always obvious exactly what you were going to get out of him—excellence, hustle, and toughness. I loved playing behind Nash because he was so selfless. If he could grab a blocker or occupy him so someone else could make a play, that's what Nash was going to do.

He was a great locker room guy as well, always regulating the pulse of the team if there was something wrong taking place. His toughness was unparalleled. I remember seeing him four days after the 1990 season in the locker room. He was nursing both of his surgically repaired elbows and had a catheter because—unbeknownst to me or anyone else—he played the last game of the year with kidney stones. He was the picture of misery, and I remember thinking, *We worked closely together on the field and were friends off the field, and I never heard him say anything about any of this.* What a tough guy!

CHAPTER 3
THE 1990S

Everything was going pretty well for me as far as my NFL career was concerned except the most frustrating part of being a professional athlete—injuries. My rookie year was followed by major offseason shoulder surgery, but from 1988 to 1989, I started 33 straight games, including a playoff game. Then a string of injuries came that would last three years. I missed the first eight games of the 1990 season, the middle 10 games of the 1991 season, and the last six games of the 1992 season. Going into the 1990 season after completing two injury-free years, I felt like the game was coming to me in a new way that I had not experienced before. Then I injured my knee, and each injury after that, I felt like I had to start over again. In my nine years of professional football, I completed just three full seasons and that—still to this day—is frustrating to me. Whenever I see a player going through what I did, my heart goes out to him.

My last year in Seattle turned out to be really fun—other than the 2–14 record and the season-ending injury in Week 10. In 1992 I was part of a top 10 defense that could've been a lot better had we not been playing with the fifth worst offense in NFL history. One game that stood out to me in particular was a game that we lost to the Raiders in Los Angeles. Defensively, if you hold a team under 300 yards, you're doing great. We held the Raiders to just 188 yards of total offense that day and lost 20–3. We actually had fun with it because our offense was so bad. The saying that year was that if you played on defense you couldn't finish an entire cup of Gatorade on the sidelines. Another suggestion was that because no team gives out gameballs after a loss, that maybe we could give out gameballs if we covered the spread.

You would think there would've been some animosity between the defense and the offense, but I never saw that happen, and from my perspective, that was because of the leadership that came from defensive coordinator Tom Catlin and head coach Tom Flores. It came close a couple of times, though. After that Raiders game, Catlin chewed us out over a lot of plays that he thought we could've made. We sat there in the darkness of the defensive meeting room and just took it. But during a bathroom break, I heard a couple of the offensive players making excuses for each other. Those excuses were coming from guys who had just put up a meager 159 yards of offense and three points!

Cortez Kennedy was the defensive MVP, and Catlin was the NFL assistant of the year. Our defense had a reputation that year, and the rest of the NFL knew when we were coming. After the game you would hear a lot of compliments from opposing players in the league. To this day I have a lot of Seahawks fans telling me how much they loved that defense. Other than Kennedy and safety Eugene Robinson, who both made the Pro Bowl, we were a bunch of no-names who played really well together. Linebacker Terry Wooden, defensive end Jeff "Boogie" Bryant, Rufus Porter, and Joe Nash were some of the unsung heroes on that defense that played as a team more than any group I've ever been around.

Things changed pretty drastically for me in 1993. I got married to former Sea Gal, Shannen Forrest, rode Plan B free agency to Denver to play for the Broncos, and within a year of that, I turned 30, and we were expecting our first child. One of the reasons I was in Denver was because of Jack Elway, who was my coach at Stanford. He was one of my favorite coaches and people in the world and was with the Broncos' personnel department back then. The Broncos probably paid me more than they wanted because of a gaping hole in a pretty solid defense. But when I got to Denver, I had the feeling they wanted a younger, cheaper player to play my position. I thought they actually might cut me to save some money.

As camp went on, I felt I could see the writing on the wall and developed a chip on my shoulder. No one there seemed to respect that I had started five years in Seattle, and a younger athletic phenom, Jeff Mills from Nebraska, was starting ahead of me in the preseason. At one point during camp in a goal-line drill, I was playing next to Mills and ran past him and made a tackle for a loss. Of all people, Jack Elway came to me and said, "We didn't know you had that kind of speed, David." I thought, *Really, Jack! Why not?*

Defensive tackle Cortez Kennedy gets in a three-point stance in 1992, the year he won Defensive Player
the Year and my last year playing for the Seahawks.

Eventually, I became the starter and had my best year as a pro, tallying 133 tackles, two sacks, an interception, and a touchdown on a fake field goal. But in the two years that followed, I would have thumb surgery, five knee surgeries, and play in just 15 games.

I don't think anyone's career ends the way they want it to. Even John Elway, who went out on top as a back-to-back Super Bowl winner and Super Bowl MVP his last year, was sobbing at the podium during his retirement press conference about how he couldn't play the way he wanted to play anymore.

I never did retire. It was just that all 30 NFL teams slammed the door in my face. I also think that most players have misgivings with their last head coach who wouldn't give them just one more chance. My last year with the Broncos was with Mike Shanahan. He cut my pay by 75 percent, which I saw coming. He gave the money he took from my contract to Dante Jones, a player who ended up starting five games at middle linebacker while I started the other 11. Shanahan had come from the Raiders organization, where Al Davis fired him and reportedly refused to pay him a quarter-million dollars. I'm not sure how you stiff someone out of money if there's a contract, but that was a well-known fact for anyone who knew Shanahan. It was also a well-known fact that Shanahan wanted to beat the Raiders in the worst way. I had a number of tackles and forced two fumbles against the Raiders, and the plays I made in those two games were instrumental in beating the Raiders twice that year in 1995.

Of the plays I made that year against the Raiders, one of them was not only my last play in the NFL, it was also critical in knocking the Raiders out of the playoffs. Going into our last game of the year, we knew that we were out of the playoffs but had one last game in Oakland on Christmas Eve of 1995. The Raiders, however, were poised to go to the playoffs if they could beat us. I had been told by the medical staff during the week before that game that I needed knee surgery. The doctors and trainers told me that I could play if I wanted to, but I definitely needed knee surgery. Outside of the examination room, Shanahan pulled me aside and said, "We really need you." So I decided to play. The game went back and forth. Late in the game that was tied at 28, James Jett caught a pass in field-goal range that would've put us away and the Raiders into the playoffs. I tackled him from behind and stripped the ball out of his hands, and we recovered. John Elway drove us down the field, and Jason Elam kicked a 37-yard field goal that knocked the Raiders out of the playoffs.

I took a 75 percent pay cut like a good soldier, watched that money go to a player who played half of the games I played in, made a number of plays in the games that he *really* wanted to win—including knocking nemesis Davis out of the playoffs—and put myself at risk playing on a knee that needed surgery. At the end of the year, he called me into his office. Was it to thank me for playing through a rough year? To invite me back to camp next year? No, it was a meeting to tell me that they were going to go another direction in the future.

Over the next two years, I had tryouts with the Minnesota Vikings, Philadelphia Eagles, and, finally, the Green Bay Packers in 1997. I still give then-Packers intern John Schneider heat for that tryout and tell him that not signing me was the biggest mistake he ever made in his NFL career. I don't remember Schneider actually being there, but I do know that Reggie McKenzie, who would later become the Raiders' general manager, gave me a ride to the airport in Green Bay. They did things like measure my hands and made me run a 40-yard dash, something I hadn't done in over 10 years, even though they had nine years of my playing film to review. Schneider is a good friend, and I kiddingly blame him for my career ending prematurely.

But in all seriousness, the writing was on the wall. When I returned home, I stretched out on our living room floor—sore from the work-out and the five 40-yard dashes I had run—and announced to my wife, "It's over."

Within two days I procured the necessary documents to file for retirement and took them to a mailing business in a strip mall in Scottsdale, Arizona. I handed the documents to the stoner behind the counter and said, "This...is my NFL retirement party." He gave me a look that said, *Whatever, dude.*

In some small part, I also think that every player thinks the game won't go on without them. In 1996 I couldn't believe that they were playing without me. It's like watching a ship loaded with your friends, family, hopes, and dreams sail away from the dock without you. I had recurring dreams for two years that some team in the NFL had an injured linebacker and needed me. I would always wake up from those dreams with a horribly empty feeling. To make it worse, the 1996 Broncos were the best team in the NFL. When they lost in the first round of the playoffs to the Jacksonville Jaguars, I popped some champagne. It was petty, I know. They won the next two Super Bowls, but it took the sting out of it that I was two years removed.

In 1998 I landed a job in wealth management with Merrill Lynch and didn't pay much attention to NFL football until 2004. If those were years of transition for me—from football player, to civilian, to finding my way back into football as an announcer—they also were for the Seahawks. They went from being a mediocre team playing in the Kingdome and playing second fiddle in Seattle to the Mariners, Sonics, and UW football to having a new stadium, hiring Mike Holmgren as coach, and being on the verge of their first Super Bowl appearance.

If the '90s marked the end of my career, they also marked the end of an era for the Seahawks. Chuck Knox was gone as coach after the 1991 season, and so was Dave Krieg. Ken Behring deciding to go with Flores, who had won two Super Bowl titles with the Raiders in the '80s, as head coach. Behring also made another critical decision that changed the fortunes of the Seahawks—and all of NFL history—forever.

In 1991 the Seahawks drafted Dan McGwire. Legend has it that Knox wanted to draft a gunslinger out of Southern Miss named Brett Favre. But Behring was smitten with McGwire, who'd been one of the big stories in college football during his senior season at San Diego State. McGwire was 6'7", had a rocket for an arm, and had a brother, Mark, who was one of the most famous baseball players in the country.

It was rumored that McGwire was a friend of the Behring family and it's well-documented that Behring was close with McGwire's agent, Leigh Steinberg, a figure who *Jerry Maguire* was loosely based on. When it was time to use the first-round pick (16th overall) in 1991, Behring got his guy. (Favre went in the second round to the Atlanta Falcons, who then infamously traded him a year later to the Green Bay Packers.) Reportedly, after that day's draft, Knox brought all of his coaches together and told them, "Gentlemen, coach your asses off this year. This might be it for us."

McGwire could not have been a more quality guy off the field. He was mature for his age and an engaging person who was articulate and even charming. With help from his brother, I'm sure, he knew how to be a pro. But on the field, I'd see him throw the ball in the dirt on the most routine throws a quarterback could make. He just looked lost in the pro game, which was surprising given the career he had in college.

In 1991 we traveled to Atlanta to play the Falcons. As we did our preparation that week, there was talk that we might see this rookie Brett Favre at some point. The Falcons weren't entirely pleased with Chris Miller, and the way coaches talked about Favre was almost legendary. Late in that game, he took some mop-up duty. His reputation as a gunslinger was well-known, and he made a move to throw the ball to a running back, whom I had a bead on. But he pulled it back at the last second. Miller yelled at me from the sidelines, "Wyman, you thought you had one, didn't you?" Favre had four attempts that year—two of them interceptions—but none of them went to me unfortunately.

My final year with the Seahawks came in 1992, the infamous 2–14 season, which was the first for Flores as coach. Making matters worse for Seattle, one of their two wins came against the New England Patriots—we all wish they'd saved a win against the Patriots for a couple decades later—which gave New England the No. 1 one pick in the 1993 draft and Seattle No. 2. And that allowed the Patriots to draft Drew Bledsoe, a quarterback out of Washington State, while Seattle got Rick Mirer, a quarterback out of Notre Dame. It was the second time in three years the Seahawks used their first-round pick on a quarterback, which is never a good sign.

The fate of the Seahawks losing out on Bledsoe, who would lead the Pats to a Super Bowl within four years, instead of Mirer has been endlessly lamented as another unfortunate turn in Seattle sports history.

While playing against the Seahawks in 1993 with my new team in Denver, one of the things I noticed, though, was that Mirer wasn't too bad. Mirer wasn't Pat Mahomes, but he did have a quiet confidence, was pretty measured, and had what I considered to be a decent rookie year. One of my two sacks that year was on him, and it was because I ran him out of bounds behind the line of scrimmage. (I did not know that was technically a sack at the time.) He was running to his left, which would've been a difficult throw and possibly an interception, but he wisely took the sack instead. He played that way his rookie year, and I thought he had a chance of developing into a good player.

Mirer actually was named to the All-NFL rookie team that season, completing 56.4 percent of his passes and throwing for 2,833 yards, though a 12:17 touchdown-to-interception ratio was a somewhat ominous foreshadowing of what was to come. Unable to replicate the success he'd had with the Raiders, Flores was fired after going 2–14, 6–10, and 6–10. The Seahawks then hired Dennis Erickson in 1995 to take his place, and it seemed like a potentially good fit on paper. Erickson was from Everett, Washington, had done a nice job at Washington State, and then led the University of Miami to two national titles. But he'd never coached in the NFL at any level and brought in a staff that also included a lot of assistants devoid of much, if any, NFL experience, and that showed throughout his tenure.

He also had issues at quarterback. Erickson benched Mirer in 1996 in favor of John Friesz, and though Erickson can be faulted for a lot of things with the Seahawks, that decision can't be questioned too much. Seattle traded Mirer the following year to the Chicago Bears for a first-round pick and a fourth rounder that the Seahawks ended up using as part of packages that landed Shawn Springs and Walter Jones in the 1997 draft. Mirer, meanwhile, went 2–13 in the rest of his career as a starter.

As I began settling into life after football, the Seahawks also tried to figure out how to navigate things in the end of the 1990s. One thing they knew they had was a budding star in Jones. Watching Big Walt play was like observing a player who had truly mastered his position. He played with a controlled violence. He never looked like he was necessarily exerting much effort, but if you watched his opponents instead, you could see the domination from the other player's perspective. You see a lot of this now in current left tackle Duane Brown. Jones never reached, lunged, or looked desperate. He was steady, and his feet were always beneath him. He almost looked calm.

But that calmness betrayed the chaos that was the Seahawks in the '90s. Behring tried to move the team to Los Angeles in 1996. He even held a few offseason workouts there and did a round of interviews with Los Angeles media. But the last thing the NFL wanted was Behring owning in the L.A. market, which was vacant after the moves of the Rams and Raiders in 1994, and that move was scuttled. The uncertainty over the team's future made the team feel somewhat rudderless for a few years, and fan support suffered as the team meandered on the field. Finally, Paul Allen came to the rescue in 1997 to buy the team from Behring and assure it would stay in Seattle once he got the funding to build a new stadium on the site of the old Kingdome.

I have been around a few owners. Much like head coaches, with the owners that I knew—John Nordstrom, Pat Bowlen, Allen—you could easily see why they are where they are. There's an it factor. After all, you have to be special in order to build $100 million or even billion dollar corporations. And then there was Behring. He was a dullard from California and became a perfect villain when he tried to move the team to L.A. He was Clay Bennett before there was Clay Bennett. And he played the role to a T before Allen entered as the knight on the white horse.

After I was done playing for the Seahawks, I went back and forth between Seattle and Scottsdale quite a bit. One of the things that stood out to me was that there were actually billboards and advertisements for Seahawks football. In the late 1980s and the early 1990s, there was no need to advertise. Those seats in the Kingdome sold themselves. I'm sure my last year, the 2–14 season, had something to do with it.

Allen had to make one more big move before really getting the franchise turned around, though. He stuck with Erickson in 1998, following an 8–8 season in 1997, in which Seattle actually had a top eight ranking in both offense and defense but kept finding inexplicable ways to lose. A 3–0 start to the 1998 season seemed like maybe Erickson had found his footing. But it wasn't to be; a losing streak ensued.

Many Seahawks fans remember Vinny Testaverde's phantom touchdown that gave the New York Jets a win against Seattle after the Seahawks blew a 15-point third-quarter lead in a December game in 1998 as the end for Erickson. Some have pointed to that call as helping spur the league to implement instant replay. If instant replay had been in effect, would Erickson have hung on another year or two? Probably not. Certainly, what happened next was the best thing for the Seahawks.

CHAPTER 4
HOLMGREN AND THE SUPER BOWL

The history of Seahawks football can be defined in five pretty clearly defined eras (or maybe four eras and one big error). There were the Jack Patera and Chuck Knox early Kingdome years; even if some of those seasons didn't have a lot of wins, things were always pretty fun and interesting. Then there was the lost decade of the '90s, a true error of an era.

The Seahawks began to come back into the light in 1999—their final year in the Kingdome but their first with Mike Holmgren as coach, a hiring that made clear that Paul Allen was serious about reviving the team. Holmgren had won a Super Bowl title with the Green Bay Packers and almost two in a row. But he wanted to run every aspect of a team, which was the one thing the Seahawks could offer that Green Bay could not. The Seahawks basically gave Holmgren an offer he couldn't refuse—an eight-year contract, in which he initially was head coach as well as executive vice president and general manager.

There was going to be no doubt that Holmgren—whom some players (I think it was Cortez Kennedy and Brian Habib) called "The Big Show"—was going to be running the whole show. The nickname eventually caught on, and you can see why Allen was so impressed by Holmgren and gave him the keys to the franchise. Holmgren is physically imposing, has a quiet wisdom, is a genius on the chalkboard, and is in command of the room. I heard Holmgren described as an artist when drawing up plays and I don't think I ever heard a cross word from him in his press conferences. He had a masterly way of dealing with both the playbook and the media, and each would serve him well as he attempted to right the ship in Seattle.

Holmgren immediately got the Seahawks to respectability with an AFC West title and a playoff berth in 1999, snapping an 11-year playoff drought. But that came with Jon Kitna at quarterback. Kitna was a solid quarterback who would go on to a long career, one that is especially admirable when placed in the context that he was an undrafted free agent out of Central Washington.

But a playoff loss to the Miami Dolphins in the final game ever played in the Kingdome and then a 6–10 record the following season made clear to Holmgren that he needed someone else running the ship to get Seattle where he really wanted it to go. It took a trade and a few backward steps along the way, but ultimately Holmgren found his guy, and the Seahawks found their way to the Super Bowl.

Holmgren knew just where to look when he wanted a new Seattle quarterback—his old team in Green Bay. About a month before the 2001 NFL Draft, the Seahawks pulled off a trade with Green Bay that by any measure has to go down as one of the best in team history. Seattle gave up its third-round pick (72nd overall) and swapped first-round picks with the Packers, allowing Green Bay to move from 17th to 10th. It could be argued that's as good of a trade as the Seahawks have ever made. Seattle took guard Steve Hutchinson with the 17th pick while Green Bay used the 10th pick on defensive end Jamal Reynolds, who played in just 18 games in his career. And with the 72nd pick, Green Bay took a linebacker named Torrance Marshall, who started just two games in a four-year career. Hutch, meanwhile, figures to make the Pro Football Hall of Fame.

After a few fits and starts, Matt Hasselbeck did indeed become the quarterback Holmgren thought he could be. If it was perfect timing for Hasselbeck to come to Seattle. He found a place where he could play early in his career, and that would have never happened while being stuck behind Brett Favre in Green Bay. Everything was about timing. The Seahawks rarely went shotgun because the ball came out micro-seconds faster with a three-step drop throw. Holmgren had the timing down so that it took longer to receive the shotgun snap, adjust the ball, and get the ball out than it did for Hasselbeck to take the snap from under center, adjust the ball so the laces were on his fingertips during his drop, hit the back step of his drop, and let the ball fly. It's something the current Seahawks could use.

Another big piece to the puzzle arrived in the 2000 when the Seahawks drafted running back Shaun Alexander in the first round out of Alabama. Seattle selected Alexander with one of the picks it got from the Dallas Cowboys in a trade for receiver Joey Galloway, who had held out the previous season. The contract stalemate and trade helped demonstrate that Holmgren was in charge and would do things his way.

He also had traded away Ahman Green that year, deciding that Green fumbled too much. In a way it was a trade of Green for Alexander because Holmgren decided he needed a young running back to help take over when Ricky Watters inevitably hit the end of the road. In terms of stats, Alexander was a huge success. During the 2005 season alone, he won the NFL MVP and scored a then-NFL record 27 rushing touchdowns.

Alexander, however, wouldn't block or catch for some reason, and this made it very predictable for opposing defenses because they pretty much knew it was a run if he was in the game. That worked when the line had Walter Jones and Hutchinson up front, but it became more of a challenge once Hutch left.

He also earned a reputation for caring about his own stats quite a bit. Alexander claimed that he was "stabbed in the back" in 2004 because the Seahawks didn't give him the ball on the 1-yard line in the last game of the year. The Seahawks were against the Atlanta Falcons, and the playoffs were on the line. Curtis Martin finished with 1,697 rushing yards (following a 153-yard game against the St. Louis Rams) to lead the NFL, while Alexander finished with 1,696. Hasselbeck executed a perfect quarterback sneak to get the Seahawks in the end zone when the Atlanta defense was thinking handoff to Alexander. (I'll never forget that coach Stump Mitchell called into our postgame show afterward and apologized for Alexander complaining about the play call and losing out on the rushing title.)

The Seahawks lost one September road game when Arizona Cardinals linebacker Gerald Hodges busted through the line on what was surely a running play. Alexander didn't want to get hit so he basically refused to take the handoff. "We just blew it," Alexander told *The Seattle Times.* "I thought Matt was audibling and then I thought, *Ah no, this is the fake audible.* And I took a step to run the play that was called and I saw the guy running in the backfield, so I thought,

Oh, maybe this is a pass play. So I go try and run around Matt, and it was crazy. I wasn't sure if he was giving it to me, if I was blocking, or if he was."

I think he said something about Keystone Cops. I remember saying in the postgame radio show that it wasn't funny. My conclusion was that he didn't want to take the hit, so he stranded Hasselbeck with the ball. It was first and 5 at the Arizona 36. If he'd just taken the handoff and took the hit like a good soldier, it would've been no worse than second and 10 from the 41. Maybe they gain 10 yards in two plays and kick a 47-yarder or at least keep it a tie game and go into overtime. Anyway, in my opinion, he made a decision that lost the game for the Seahawks.

But there was, of course, plenty of good stuff about Alexander, too. He was a saint off the field. And then there are the numbers. You can debate who was most responsible for the team's great running game in that era—Jones, Hutch, and the line or Alexander. But somebody has to run the ball—and do so in the manner that the demanding Holmgren wanted. Alexander left Seattle with 9,429 yards, almost 2,700 more than Chris Warren, who is in second place. He had five touchdowns in a game against the Minnesota Vikings in 2002 (all in the first half). That team record of 30 points may also be really hard for anyone else to ever top.

And there was that MVP season in 2005. It felt like when he got paid big money in 2006, it was for what he had done—not what he was about to do. I thought that it was a mistake, and that's the kind of "pay for the past, not the future" contract that Pete Carroll and John Schneider have really tried to avoid. Alexander pretty much surrendered every time he got hit and he would always choose running out of bounds over taking a hit. He was the anti-Marshawn Lynch. You could also argue that's how he stayed healthy and was able to get the yards that he did. It's undeniable that Alexander is one of the great all-time Seahawks, but I still think they should've paid Hutch instead.

The year before Alexander won the MVP, the 2004 Seahawks won the NFC West with a 9–7 record. Two of those seven losses were to their nemesis in the division, the Rams, including a heartbreaking loss to St. Louis in Week 5. They led the Rams 27–10 in the fourth quarter and then gave up the lead and lost in overtime 33–27. After they won the division, they again hosted the Rams in a wild-card game. Somehow, they lost for a third time that year to what was the last remnants of "The Greatest Show on Turf." That loss came when Hasselbeck failed to connect with Bobby Engram, his most reliable receiver, from the 5-yard line with 27 seconds left.

That season was the second straight year Seattle had made the play-offs and was just the franchise's third division title. Despite that success there was some angst in Seattle that Holmgren had yet to really win big. And following the 2002 season when the Seahawks went just 7–9 and missed the playoffs for the third straight season, Holmgren surrendered his general manager duties. Getting back to the postseason in 2003 helped placate the fanbase some and also seemed to show that coaching was what Holmgren did best. But devastating playoff losses in 2003 (the "we want the ball and we're going to score" game at Green Bay) and 2004 had everyone still a little on edge and set up the 2005 season as a big one for Holmgren.

Going into the 2005 season, though, it seemed like there was a lot to like with maybe the best offensive line in the NFL and maybe the best running back. But the defense needed to come on. In 2004 the Seahawks gave up an average of 32 points in their seven losses and they needed help defensively. It arrived in the draft in the form of two good linebackers, Leroy Hill and Lofa Tatupu, who helped to transform a defense that would go on to allow 102 points fewer in 2005 than in 2004.

Seattle finished 13–3 that season, winning 11 in a row at one point. But it may be forgotten now that they started that season 2–2, including road losses to the Jacksonville Jaguars and Washington Redskins. Then in Week 5 they traveled to take on the dastardly Rams, who also were 2–2. St. Louis ran back the opening kickoff for a touchdown, but then something clicked. Seattle rallied to win 37–31 to start that

11-game winning streak that remains the best in franchise history. The Seahawks didn't lose again until the final game of the year when the No. 1 seed and home-field advantage was already locked up.

Two monumental wins that year indicated that this was a special team that was meant for greatness, and they came in back-to-back games. In Week 11 the Seahawks hosted the New York Giants, and kicker Jay Feely missed three field goals that all could have given the Giants—who statistically outplayed Seattle that day, gaining 490 yards—the win. One missed kick came with four seconds left in regulation, and two more occurred in overtime. Perhaps because those errant kicks occurred while playing for a team in New York, Feely's foibles that day were immortalized in a *Saturday Night Live* skit. It was about him having to land a plane between two radio towers. (Spoiler alert: it doesn't go so well.)

Josh Brown kicked the game-winner in overtime with 2:49 left on the clock to give the Seahawks their seventh straight win. The next week they went on the road for a *Monday Night Football* game against the Philadelphia Eagles. There had been some skepticism that the Seahawks had merely feasted on a weak NFC West and had simply benefited from the three missed field goals the week before against a Giants team that some thought was the best in the conference. But in what was maybe the best performance to date by a Holmgren team, the Seahawks destroyed the Eagles, taking a 35–0 halftime lead thanks to two defensive touchdowns from their two rookie linebackers, Tatupu and Hill. In addition to forcing a fumble, Hill also had one-and-a-half sacks and six tackles. Tatupu led the team in tackles with nine, picked off a pass for a touchdown, and broke up four passes. The Seahawks announced themselves to the world that night on the biggest stage.

In that memorable 42–0 win against the Eagles, Tatupu not only had the pick-6, but he also tipped another pass that was intercepted by safety Michael Boulware. They were two great plays, no matter how you look at it. But talking to him afterward about those two plays is what blew me away and was a testament to Tatupu's over-the-top understanding of the game—even as a rookie—and a good lesson for everyone that what you see on Sunday isn't always as simple as it may seem.

On both plays the Seahawks were in Cover-2, which is one of the dominant defensive schemes of modern football and is a defense where you cover the deep part of the field with your two safeties and drop five players into the underneath zones. The best way for an offense to put pressure on a defense playing Cover-2 is with your tight end or wide receivers running vertical or go routes—meaning, going deep—down the middle of the field. This forces linebackers to have to run downfield to help the two safeties, who are covering half of the field. Because a defense is susceptible to vertical routes like that, a lot of offenses will run a stick route or just a quick out. Offensively, you try to persuade the linebacker in the middle of the field to turn his hips and run down the field. Once the receiver gets that from you, he jabs his foot in the ground, makes a quick out move, and it's typically good for about a 12 to 15-yard reception. That's what the Eagles ran, and Tatupu bravely (especially for a rookie) jumped the stick route and picked off the pass for a 38-yard interception for a touchdown.

The counter to that is to run a "Y Stick Nod," which means the tight end runs the stick route and then jabs his foot in the ground a second time and continues vertically down the field. It's basically a double move. The Eagles offensive coordinator ran that play two series later in an attempt to victimize a rookie linebacker who took a chance earlier. Only Tatupu didn't bite on it. He laid off of the stick route and continued downfield and tipped the ball in the air that ended up in Boulware's hands. "Because I jumped the stick route and picked it off, I knew they were going to come back with the stick nod," he told me, "and try to get me to jump the stick again and burn me deep."

He knew it was coming! The rookie linebacker outsmarted offensive coordinator Brad Childress and head coach Andy Reid, each of whom is among the best in recent NFL history. (Reid is now among the top 10 head coaches in terms of wins in the history of the league.)

Head coach Mike Holmgren patrols the sideline in 2006 as the Seahawks defeat the Carolina Panthers 34–14 in the NFC Championship Game.

To have that understanding of the game as a rookie is something I'd never heard of then and haven't since except for maybe the things I hear Kam Chancellor and Richard Sherman talk about.

Tatupu is one of my all-time favorite Seahawks. He and I were selected in the same spot for the same team—Tatupu was the 45th overall pick in the second round—and we were both linebackers. We also both came from the Pac-10. Tatupu played for Pete Carroll at USC where he was a standout on their 2004 national title team. I had even met Tatupu when he was five years old. I played in a golf tournament with his father, Mosi Tatupu (a former NFL player), and I met him in the Boston airport when he wore a football jersey and sported a mohawk (typical linebacker).

But that's where the similarities ended. In 2007 Tatupu matched my career total in interceptions in a single game.

Tatupu liked playing against the Eagles apparently. Two years later in the 2007 season, he picked off three passes against the Eagles. I interviewed him after the game and told him I was mad at him because he bested me in just one game. His response was, "Well, I appreciate it, but I could've had four!"

That's another common characteristic of the really good players. They only remember the plays they didn't make. It's a tortured existence.

Sadly, 2010 would be the last year for Tatupu in Seattle. For a player with that knowledge of the game and that much talent, six years was way too short. But during the time he played, it was clear that he was made to play the game.

Anyway, as good as the offense was in 2005—Alexander won the MVP award, and Jones and Hutchinson formed one of the best left sides of an offensive line in NFL history—the defense had more to do with that 13–3 team than people think.

The Seahawks' best NFC record set up a favorable path to the Super Bowl: win two games and head to Detroit. Those two wins ultimately came fairly easily—by NFL playoff standards anyway—against the Washington Redskins and Carolina Panthers. Getting the win against the Panthers at home was as big of a moment in Seattle sports history as any other. (The 1979 Sonics won the NBA title on the road, and the Mariners have never been to a World Series).

The excitement in the city was over the top for the Seahawks as they prepared to play the Pittsburgh Steelers in the Super Bowl. And since I was back working in media in Seattle, I got to experience it all firsthand. It was fun to take part in the phenomenon that is Radio Row at the Super Bowl. I sat in the stands for the game, and Seattle's 21–10 loss is now remembered mostly for a few bad calls that went against the Seahawks. For those of us who were at the game, the bad calls didn't really resonate that much in the immediate moment. Maybe it's being caught up in the atmosphere, or that they didn't really play the replays in the stadium that much.

To be sure, the Seahawks could have done some things to help themselves, but the calls stand out. There was the phantom push off by receiver Darrell Jackson in the end zone to negate a touchdown. That was the worst to me. His arm moved like a push off, but you could see it didn't have that effect on the defender. Then there the was the touchdown that wasn't scored by Ben Roethlisberger. And then the bizarre call on Hasselbeck blocking below the waist on an interception return.

Even with all of those bad calls, what sunk the Seahawks that day was a play with about 11 minutes left in the second quarter. Up to that point, the Seahawks defense had allowed just 17 yards and forced three three-and-outs. But on third and 8, the Steelers ran a reverse that more than doubled their yardage for the game. The problem was that free safety Marquand Manuel made the tackle and slipped on the third-down marker on the sidelines and blew out his groin.

Manuel was the second-string safety because Ken Hamlin had nearly been killed in a bar fight after the Houston Texans game earlier in the year. So now they were down to their third-string safety, Etric Pruitt. If the backside of the defense had stayed home and checked reverse before flying over to the front side of the play, there might be a totally different result in that game.

Back in Seattle, no one could get over the injustice of the bad calls. Even Holmgren addressed it at the pep rally back at Qwest Field, famously saying, "I knew we were gonna have to play the Steelers. I didn't know we were gonna have to play the refs, too."

The hope when he said that was that the Seahawks were going to get a pretty quick chance at revenge. Instead, it took a few years—and a couple of coaching changes—before Seattle had another opportunity to win it all.

It's too bad that the Seahawks couldn't keep their offensive line together after 2005 to see what could have been. When people think about Jones, they think about pass blocking and protecting the quarterback's blind side. But I remember watching him block on a running play, and something odd happened. I swore the defender's head popped up like a Rock 'Em Sock 'Em robot. When I went back and looked at the play later, Jones had gotten under a 275-pound Atlanta Falcons defensive end and picked him up off the ground and drove him several yards down field. The play was indicative of just how dominant the Seattle offensive line was in that era.

But Seattle lost Hutchinson via free agency to the Vikings, though it was hardly just that simple. (The phrase "poison pill" will always be a curse word to Seahawks fans.) First of all, they should've just paid Hutch. No franchise tag, no funny business—just freaking pay him. I, however, blame the NFL for this one. The spirit of the transition tag, which Seattle placed on Hutchinson instead of immediately giving him a long-term deal, was that the team would have a chance to match.

But that was also on Hutch because he ultimately allowed his agent Tom Condon to put that verbiage in the contract. I don't blame Hutch, though. They gave a huge fat contract to Alexander that I knew was a waste. His yardage went down 50 percent every year after that, and part of that was because he didn't have Hutchinson blocking for him.

The Seahawks still managed division titles in 2006 and 2007, giving them four in a row, and even had a memorable playoff win in 2006 when a young Dallas Cowboys quarterback named Tony Romo couldn't handle a snap on a potential game-winning field goal. But it was clear the team was trending downward after the glory of the 2005 season and it all came to a thud in 2008 when Hasselbeck got hurt, and Seattle went 4–12.

It was tough to watch a Holmgren team struggle like that after watching them win four straight division titles. It was tough to watch Hasselbeck struggle, too. For a while there, Holmgren and Hasselbeck worked so well together. The 2005 season was the pinnacle; the 2008 season was the bottom.

Hasselbeck completed just 52 percent of his passes while playing just seven games. Seattle went 1–6 in his starts that season, and he threw twice as many interceptions (10) as touchdowns (five).

CHAPTER 5
2009 AND FROM MORA TO CARROLL

The Mike Holmgren era was going to be a tough one to top. But the Seahawks thought (or hoped) they had a ready-made succession plan with the hiring of Jim Mora in 2009 after he had been hired in 2008 as a coach-in-waiting. Mora had seemed like to the perfect head coach to fill in after Holmgren. He coached under him in 2008–09 as defensive backs coach and assistant head coach and was waiting in the wings for the head coaching job. He was initially a popular choice. He'd been a favored son at UW, many UW fans wanted him hired there, and his time with the Seahawks looked good at first.

Mora was great with the media. There were times though that I thought he was almost too honest. Usually coaches communicate in some cryptic form of discussion that doesn't really tell you anything. But Mora wasn't afraid to speak his mind—even when it could come back to really bite him.

When he was the head coach of the Atlanta Falcons, he did an interview on a sports station in Seattle. Asked about the coaching job at his alma mater Washington, then held by Tyrone Willingham, he indicated that he would be open to coaching the Huskies. "If [Willingham] decides he's ready to move on, and they want me, I will be there," Mora said. "I don't care if we're in the middle of a playoff run. I'm packing my stuff and going back to Seattle."

Mora reportedly had to apologize to his bosses in Atlanta. And Mora's mouth made for some memorable moments with the Seahawks. The best example was after the Chicago Bears game, in which kicker Olindo Mare—at the time regarded as one of the best in the game (heading into the 2019 season, he ranked 19th all time in made field goals)—missed two field goals in a 29–25 loss. Mora called the performance "not acceptable." "We'll look at changes everywhere," Mora said. "We're not going to fight our ass off and have a field-goal kicker miss two field goals. It's not going to happen."

He later sort of apologized and backtracked a bit. "When the question was directed at me, I answered it honestly but probably with just a little bit too much…um…you fill in the word," he said.

I really liked Mora. He seemed like a great choice, and I was sad to see that it didn't work out for him. I remember him chasing first-round draft choice Aaron Curry out on to the field, yelling at him the entire way. I liked that he didn't seem to treat his players differently, but yelling at your grown-up football players might be part of the evidence that he lost that team by the end of the year. Some coaches can pull it off and some can't.

A Butkus Award-winning linebacker out of Wake Forest who the Seahawks chose with the fourth overall pick of the 2009 draft, Curry was possibly more disappointing than the season itself. Other top five picks in Seahawks history were transcendent players like Cortez Kennedy, Curt Warner, and Kenny Easley. He looked like the safest bet at the time, and you could see in college that Curry could play.

He was physically dominant. He was an all-muscle, 6'2", 250-pound hitting machine. A number of times, he hit a tight end, a running back, or even a 320-pound offensive lineman, and those players limped off the field or got up slowly. He could run and hit. But there was something clogging his brain. My Denver Broncos linebacker coach, John Paul Young, had a saying when you would do something odd or dumb: "You need to take out your brain and wash it!" I thought about that every time I watched Curry play.

The best (or worst) example of that occurred in a game against the Falcons that year. He clearly had man-to-man coverage on a tight end. The tight end ran a crossing pattern, and so Curry ran with him, staying right in his hip pocket. It was great coverage, but it was a running play, and as he was focusing in on his coverage, he ran right past the running back with the ball. He could've reached out and at least slowed the ball carrier—if not tackled him for a minimal gain. But he never even realized or acknowledged that it was a run and not a pass.

I have an interesting yet ridiculous exercise I like to indulge myself with. It involves unscrewing one player's head and screwing it on top of another player's body. Example: if I could screw Dave Krieg's head on top of Dan McGwire's body, I would have the perfect Seahawks quarterback. McGwire was 6'7" and had a rocket for an arm but couldn't complete a simple five-yard swing pattern to a running back. Krieg was 6'1", he came from a school (Milton College) that is now a parking lot, he had small hands, and you could record his 40-yard dash on a calendar. But he played 19 years in the NFL, threw for more than 38,000 yards, and I believe he is a Hall of Fame quarterback.

So, if I could screw Lofa Tatupu's head on top of Curry's body, I believe I would have the perfect linebacker. Tatupu was the smartest football player I've ever watched.

There are three parts to a football play. You must get lined up in the proper position to execute your assignment, execute your assignment and fulfill your responsibility for your coach and your teammates, and finally turn it loose and be a football player. Sadly, Curry was missing part three, and that did nothing to help Mora out in a season, in which he needed all the help he could get.

* * *

After a somewhat optimistic beginning in 2009, Seattle started out 2–3 with shutouts of the Jacksonville Jaguars and St. Louis Rams, but things went haywire toward the end of the 2009 season. The Seahawks lost their last four games to finish 5–11, three of which were pretty uncompetitive—34–7 at the Houston Texans, 24–7 at home against a Tampa Bay Buccaneers team that finished 3–13, and 48–10 at the Green Bay Packers.

But while there was a lot of grumbling at the end of the season, no one really thought Mora would get just one year with the Seahawks. And the team seemed to indicate he'd be back when he was allowed to hold a season-ending press conference and talk about his plans for the future. But in one of the more stunning turnabouts in team history, Mora was indeed fired, and a surprising name—Pete Carroll—replaced him.

When they fired Mora and announced the hiring of Carroll, I thought, *They're getting the same guy*. True, Carroll was an amazingly successful college coach at USC. Had the Trojans not lost in overtime to Cal in 2003, his 34-game winning streak could have been 38, and the streak could've been 48 had they not lost to Washington State in overtime in 2002. Over a stretch between 2002 and 2007, his won-loss record at USC was 69–8. But as an NFL coach, he was barely a .500 coach with a record of 33–31 during one season with the New York Jets (1994) and three with the New England Patriots (1997–99). With the Patriots he was the coach who bridged the tenures of coaching luminaries Bill Parcells and Bill Belichick.

His college and pro records seemed to confirm that he was a perfect coach for college football, and both his message and coaching style were a college approach, not a pro football approach. But Carroll won me over with his very first press conference with the media in Seattle. He seemed to be very self-aware, and you got the feeling that he not only had a firm grasp of what went right at USC, but also of what went wrong in New England and New York. And with that said, a winning record as a head coach in the NFL (33–31) is nothing to scoff at. His enthusiasm and positivity seemed very rah-rah in the beginning, but when he explained his philosophy, you couldn't help but buy in. I'm not sure that my perception of any one person was flip-flopped more than my perception of Carroll.

Pairing Carroll with John Schneider as the team's next general manager was the next stroke of genius by the Seahawks. Schneider got hired in a slightly unconventional way because Carroll essentially interviewed the general manager candidates. General managers are often the bosses of a team's coach, but in this case, Carroll was hiring Schneider to work with him at the top of the organization. (Carroll has always had the title of executive vice president of football operations with the Seahawks.) Maybe not every NFL coach or GM could make such an arrangement work, but I sensed immediately that this one might.

When Schneider first came to Seattle, he called me and asked me to come in and talk to his scouts and personnel people. I remember thinking, *What do you want from me?* When I got to the facility, Jacob Green and Hall of Fame quarterback Warren Moon were both there, too. He had asked them to do the same thing. He asked me my thoughts about the character of the successful players I played with, what stood out about them, and what made them good players. Like Carroll, Schneider never gave you the impression that he had it all figured out. There was an open curiosity and humility that ran through their approach. Most of the times that I see Schneider, he is carrying a notebook, and when he asks me questions about my career and the different players and coaches I played with, he often scribbles down notes in the notebook, always trying to make himself—and by extension, the Seahawks—better. I've observed that intelligent and successful people have more questions than answers. Carroll and Schneider are just like that. Though the road the Seahawks took to get to a pairing of Carroll/Schneider had been a little circuitous, the franchise was again on the right path.

CHAPTER 6
2010 SEASON

The end of Jim Mora and the hiring of Pete Carroll and John Schneider meant the beginning of not only a new era in Seahawks football, but also the best era of Seahawks football. Carroll was officially hired on January 11, 2010, and Schneider was brought in eight days later.

Carroll and Schneider got right to work. There were hundreds of transactions, including moves like trading for Chris Clemons, who would prove to be a key player in Carroll's defense as the Leo or weakside defensive end. But the 2010 draft is where they set a course for what would be a legendary defense and set the foundation for all that was to come.

Carroll and Schneider arrived to find one big gift—thanks to a trade with the Denver Broncos in 2009. Denver so urgently wanted to move up in the second round to take cornerback Alphonso Smith that it gave Seattle a first-round choice. If your reaction is to ask, "Who is Alphonso Smith?" Well, that's sort of the point.

With their own pick in the first round (No. 6 overall), the Seahawks took left tackle Russell Okung. Then they had to wait eight agonizing picks before being able to take a free safety named Earl Thomas from Texas with the pick they got from the Broncos.

Other players of note in that draft included receiver Golden Tate from Notre Dame, cornerback Walter Thurmond III from Oregon, and tight end Anthony McCoy of USC. All would go on to contribute to the team's success. But as good as all of those picks were, none of them had the impact on the culture of the Seahawks like their fifth-round pick, safety Kam Chancellor. He came from Virginia Tech, where he had originally been recruited as a quarterback.

It was not just Chancellor's play that stood out. It was his presence on the field and his quiet leadership off the field. There were stories that he and Thomas would watch hours and hours of film together, and they played as if they had played together for years. A decade later when you look at Chancellor's stats, maybe they don't blow you away.

But some of the plays on the field do. It was the hits he would make—like the one on Demaryius Thomas in Super Bowl XLVIII that set the tone for the entire game. He also delivered the hit on Vernon Davis on the goal line against the San Francisco 49ers in a rollicking 42–13 win in 2012 that took away his heart and his soul.

Unfortunately, Chancellor was a rookie when the NFL started cracking down on violent hits on the field, something that was his specialty. He wasn't making a lot of money as a fifth rounder, and at one point, I thought Chancellor's fines might be more than his pay. Chancellor, though, would someday get his money.

Not every move Carroll and Schneider made turned into gold. In the NFL no one bats .1000, and it's fair to say Carroll and Schneider started out 0–1. In what was regarded as its first significant move, Seattle traded with the San Diego Chargers to acquire quarterback Charlie Whitehurst and then immediately signed him to a two-year, $8 million contract. This was when the Seahawks still had Matt Hasselbeck on the roster. But Carroll and Schneider knew they'd have to move on from Hasselbeck sooner rather than later and at the time they didn't rule out that Whitehurst could be the quarterback of the future.

It was a struggle at quarterback for Carroll and Schneider those first couple of years. I did not like the trade. I've never seen a player that was so content to be a backup. Whitehurst clearly wasn't the answer, and they would go from Hasselbeck to Whitehurst to Tarvaris Jackson over the next two years. Whitehurst was gone by the end of the 2011 season, having started only four games—or $2 million per start. Seattle didn't really get its money's worth, going 1–3 in those starts, though the one win was at least a good one—the season finale in 2010 that sent Seattle to the playoffs.

Carroll's first year seemed like it was put together with bailing wire and duct tape. Though the Seahawks went 7–9, there were some early signs of life. They blew out the 49ers in Week 1, which included a Marcus Trufant interception for a touchdown. And in Week 3, they beat the Chargers 27–20 because of two kickoff returns for a touchdown from Leon Washington.

And then at 2–2, they had a bye week in which they traded with the Buffalo Bills for a former first-round pick running back named Marshawn Lynch.

Carroll was well aware of Lynch from his days coaching at USC when Lynch was terrorizing the Pac-10 at Cal. And if the Bills appeared to already have tired of Lynch, giving him up for a fourth-round and fifth-round pick, it didn't take long to realize he'd be a good fit in Seattle. It was well-known that Carroll wanted to run the ball, and after seeing Lynch run the ball in a game against the Chicago Bears, you could see there was something special there.

Interestingly, Lynch was a different person then—far from the "I'm just here so I don't get fined" guy. I was in on one of the first interviews when he came to town. When radio host Dave Grosby asked him the first question, his eyes got big, and he said, "Whoa...I did *not* expect that voice to come out of your body!" He was talkative and jovial. He laughed and smiled a lot. He told us about his lack of familiarity with snow as a rookie: "Up in Buffalo they got this stuff called slush! I grew up in Oakland, man...what is slush?" After the Chicago game, a reporter named Jon Saraceno started asking him questions, and when he looked up and saw that Saraceno sort of looked like Charlie Whitehurst, he took a hilarious double take and yelled out, "Man I thought you were Charlie! Yo, Charlie, is this your pops over here?" He was fun and happy like Michael Bennett and Richard Sherman were in the early days.

In that first game in Chicago, Lynch was not the leading rusher. He only had 44 yards and a 2.6-yard average. But you could see that there was no one like him in the league. He had some of the most spectacular zero and one-yard gains I had ever seen. There would be three or four tacklers on his back, and he would simply refuse to go down. He ran with an attitude that suggested you better bring everything you got if you wanted to tackle him.

He never cracked the 100-yard mark that year, but he was such a punishing runner, and that was something Carroll wanted out of his running game. As a former defender, I can attest to the fact that it's one thing to have a team pass on you up and down the field. But it's another when a team physically wears you down with the run, and that's what Carroll wanted.

The Seahawks went into the last game of the year with a record of 6–9 and knew that if they beat the St. Louis Rams, they would win the NFC West. They had just come off of a horrible 38–15 loss to the Tampa Bay Buccaneers. LeGarrette Blount ran for 164 yards and went over them, around them, and through them; on one play he hurdled Lawyer Milloy. It did not look like a division-winning team.

Against the Bucs, Hasselbeck also had a one-yard run for a touchdown, in which he pulled his butt muscle. So he was out for the game that would determine the playoffs. Somehow they beat a 7–8 Rams team 16–6 in a game that was indicative of how bad the NFC West was that year. But as much fun as a lot of people nationally wanted to make of the Seahawks reaching the playoffs at 7–9, it also led to one of the most memorable moments in team history—and yet another early sign that the Carroll years were never going to be boring.

Winning the division—at 7–9 or not—meant Seattle got to host a playoff game. And that came against none other than the defending Super Bowl champion New Orleans Saints, who despite being 11–5, which included a rout of Seattle earlier in the season, had to come to CenturyLink Field. No one nationally thought Seattle had much of a chance. The Seahawks were the biggest home underdog in NFL playoff history, as the Saints were favored by 10 points.

But with Hasselbeck back at the helm, the Seahawks had a surprising outburst of offense. Hasselbeck threw four touchdowns, and the Seahawks took a 24–17 lead just before half and never lost it. With about nine minutes left in the game, the Saints pulled within 34–30 and needed a stop on defense.

That's when Lynch made a play that was recorded by a Richter scale and would be recorded in Seahawks lore forever. On second and 10, Lynch ran 67 yards for a touchdown that took the gas out of the Saints, but there was so much more in that run than that sentence reveals.

The pulling guard, Mike Gibson, made a great block and so did fullback Michael Robinson. Lynch did the rest, dodging, weaving, and plowing his way through the Saints' defense, breaking at least six tackles and then diving over the goal line while holding his crotch.

The best part of the run came when he stiff-armed safety Tracy Porter to the ground. Lynch appeared to almost go backward while pushing him down and somehow regained his momentum. The length of the run led to one of the longest extended roars in Seahawks history,

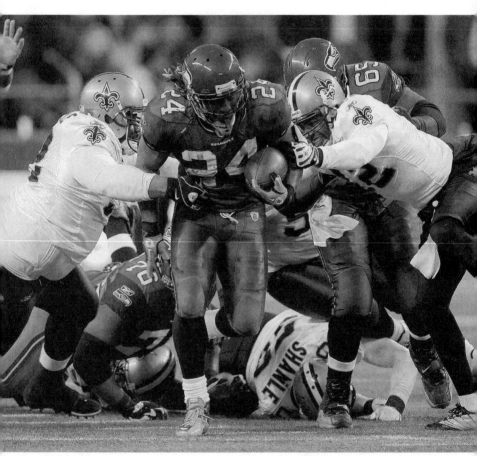

Running back Marshawn Lynch breaks several tackles during the "Beast Quake" run against the New Orleans Sa

which only grew in intensity as Lynch broke tackle after tackle. It grew so loud that a seismometer a block away showed vibrations during the run. That ended up giving the play its memorable name—the "Beast Quake" run.

I was in the press box for that game, and as it shook, a familiar feeling came over me. In 2001 I was working at Merrill Lynch, and my office was on the 24th floor of an office building in Bellevue, Washington, during the Nisqually earthquake, which measured at 6.8. It felt like that building was going to tip over. That's what it felt like in the press box that night. The roar of the crowd made it feel even worse—or better.

There are some underrated things about Marshawn Lynch, but his ability to go from stop to go and to regain his momentum from a standstill was probably his best attribute. Also, I don't think he got enough credit for his burst and speed. But that's because he sought contact downfield. He was not a breakaway runner. As powerful and as strong as Lynch was, his feet were amazing. This is something you see in most great football players like Lynch and Walter Jones—they're light on their feet and always able to keep their feet underneath them.

Lynch called a play like that "Beast Mode." "You can't just say, 'I wanna go Beast Mode. I wanna go Beast Mode,'" Lynch said. "It don't work like that. Beast Mode has to be inside of you."

That Beast Mode got a 7–9 team to the next round of the playoffs against the Bears, and the Seahawks lost 35–24 in a game they were never really in. They scored three fourth-quarter touchdowns, but the Lance Briggs and Brian Urlacher-led Bears defense allowed just 34 yards rushing and held Lynch to just four yards before he left the game early with an injury. But his run the previous week spoke loudly about where the Seahawks were headed.

CHAPTER 7

2011 AND THE BIRTH OF THE LEGION OF BOOM

The move into the 2011 season was painful to watch. Pete Carroll had certainly gotten it done in his first year with a division title—as unlikely as it was—and a playoff team that at least got the city buzzing again about the Seahawks. It was a time when the city needed someone to root for. The Sonics were gone, the Mariners were in their seemingly endless doldrums, and the UW football team was still trying to find its way out of its mid-2000s lull.

But when they wanted to move on from Matt Hasselbeck and Lofa Tatupu during that offseason, I didn't like it. Hasselbeck was a free agent, so they elected to go with Charlie Whitehurst and newly signed Tarvaris Jackson as their quarterbacks. Both were on two-year deals for $4 million a season, though one would prove to be a lot more overpaid than the other. Additionally, Tatupu did not want to restructure his $4 million-plus contract, so he and the Seahawks agreed to part ways.

That meant the quarterback of the offense and the defense for the past five years, who had each been such key parts of the franchise's first Super Bowl appearance, were gone—and rather unceremoniously so—with no evidence that they would be easily replaced. But it pretty quickly became apparent in a number of ways that Carroll and Schneider knew what they were doing.

They not only continued the revamping of the roster in Year Two, but also the coaching staff, specifically on the offensive side. One major change was hiring Tom Cable as offensive line coach, which would prove to be enormously successful in some ways but ultimately also prove to lead to a lot of controversy down the road. Cable, whom they brought in from the Oakland Raiders, could coach the run game. The Raiders had the No. 2 running game the year before he arrived in Seattle, rushing for 155 yards per game. But in something that would foreshadow how things would go for Cable in Seattle, that same line allowed 44 sacks, which was fifth worst in the league.

While Cable was hired to fix the run game, Carroll also brought in Darrell Bevell as offensive coordinator and to oversee the passing game. Bevell, who had worked with Brett Favre with the Green Bay

Packers and also with the Minnesota Vikings, replaced Jeremy Bates, who came from USC with Carroll and lasted just one year. Under Bates the offense ranked 28th in the NFL. What Carroll really wanted out of his offense was to run the ball, and despite the Beast Quake run and some flashes of brilliance from Marshawn Lynch, the Seahawks averaged just 89 yards rushing per game in 2010. With the way Carroll wanted to play, that was going to have to change.

What was unclear in that second season was whether the Seahawks had a quarterback to get the team where Carroll really wanted to go. One thing was clear about Jackson: he was a great backup quarterback. But as the Seahawks learned, he wasn't a starter. And if it came down to it, he couldn't win a game in the fourth quarter for you.

In the beginning of the 2011 season, the Seahawks started off 0–2, and everybody was calling for T-Jack's head. They wanted Whitehurst. But at that point, the rest of the team wasn't giving him much help. They had the worst running game in the league, averaging under 50 yards per game. Jackson had gotten hit and sacked more than any other quarterback other than Jay Cutler. He had thrown just one interception, which was a prescribed Hail Mary at the end of a half, and he was two dropped passes (Lynch and Ben Obomanu) from being a 65 percent passer.

Two games later in a home game against the Atlanta Falcons, he had a chance to engineer a game-winning drive when the team was down by three points. He got the offense past the 50-yard line, but in the end, the Seahawks ended up attempting a 61-yard field goal by Stephen Hauschka, which was about 10 yards beyond anything Hauschka was capable of.

That was the case with Jackson, and it's what makes him one of the more tragic characters in Seahawks history. T-Jack could get you to .500, could steady the ship, but he could not engineer a comeback win. I call it "tragic" because he was arguably the most beloved teammate in team history or at least since I've been around the team. Everybody from defensive linemen to receivers loved T-Jack both on and off the field.

When a plucky rookie named Russell Wilson got the starting job the next year, there were still those on the team who felt T-Jack deserved the job. One reason so many teammates felt so strongly about T-Jack was because he had played through so much pain in 2011, particularly through a sternum bruise that made it hard to handle the most obvious task of a quarterback—throwing. That was among the many injuries he got from being hit so often.

I've learned to listen to the players when you're talking about teammates. When you interview players, they have a tendency to refer to their teammates—the good ones anyway. The praise of Jackson came from nearly every player you talked to.

Every player in NFL history who is not wearing a gold jacket comes to the sad realization that he has limits. Jackson's limit was that he couldn't win a game that was on the line. He was tough as hell, played through all kinds of injuries, was a good NFL quarterback, but did not have the qualities that a soon-to-be drafted quarterback has.

* * *

I actually don't believe in lockdown corners and, having watched Richard Sherman in college, I had no idea what the Seahawks were thinking when they took him in the fifth round of the 2011 draft. Since I played at Stanford, I watched Stanford football pretty closely, and he was the player I talked about the most to my fellow Stanford football fans.

There was a lot of complaining. *"Sherman got beat again." "What in the hell was he thinking?" "They should move him back to receiver."* On and on the discussion went about Sherman during his college days.

So I saw nothing to indicate he might someday be a guy who would be at the forefront of the turnaround of the Seahawks. Yet when I think about the amazing players that Pete Carroll and John Schneider have pulled out of the later rounds, Sherman is the ultimate diamond in the rough. Carroll, of course, had seen Sherman play up close and personal a few times during his USC coaching career, and for those who have long thought Carroll's familiarity with college players helped Seattle's great drafting from 2010 to 2012, Sherman is Exhibit A.

In fact, Carroll had tried to recruit Sherman, who grew up within an eyelash of the Los Angeles Memorial Coliseum. The two were on the same flight to the Senior Bowl and "talked a little bit," Sherman said. In one of their most famous wheeler-dealer moves, the Seahawks got Sherman in a pick they acquired in a trade involving multiple picks with the Detroit Lions. (The Seahawks used the other picks on John Moffitt, Kris Durham, and Pep Livingston, who were all long gone by the time the 2013 Super Bowl arrived, but one proved to be enough in this case.)

As I began watching him closely with the Seahawks, my admiration for Sherman's game grew. He is simply amazing with his hands and practically never misses a jam at the line of scrimmage. His understanding of the game and what opposing offenses are trying to do to beat him is superior, and in my mind, he is the best tackling cornerback in NFL history.

Another piece of the Legion of Boom came into place in 2011 as Kam Chancellor moved into the starting lineup for good, and veteran Lawyer Milloy moved on. Chancellor was an incredibly versatile player for a strong safety; maybe it was that high school quarterback background at work.

I was worried for Chancellor because you could see he was a ferocious football player and a pure hitter. Since the NFL was trying to cut down on helmet-to-helmet hits, I was left wondering if maybe he was too rough for the game of football nowadays. That season Chancellor was flagged for two penalties that stood out, and that made me wonder if he was a player meant for another era in the NFL. In a game against the Cleveland Browns, he was penalized for unnecessary roughness on a sack that he made on Colt McCoy. The other was in the Baltimore Ravens game when he hit wide receiver Anquan Boldin, arguably one of the toughest receivers of all time, on a seam route. He ended up hurting himself on the hit while Boldin jumped right up. (This is how inconsistently they call that penalty. Typically, if the receiver gets right up, there is no flag.) Nevertheless, Chancellor was a punisher, and there was now enough film out there that made receivers think twice when running crossing patterns. His coverage, I always thought, could be a liability at times. But the hits—and the run defense—more than made up for it.

Chancellor would be the first of the Legion of Boom to get a second contract from the Seahawks. Seattle awarded him that deal, a four-year, $28 million contract, a few months before the 2013 season. Carroll and Schneider didn't have to worry how Chancellor would react to new-found riches; he famously used his money to buy his mother a new home as his first purchase. He not only played up to every cent of that contract, but his coverage, which I thought might've been suspect, also became the best part of his game.

When Brandon Browner, the final piece of the Legion of Boom, first showed up to camp in July of 2011, I mistook him for a defensive end. Soon enough, we'd find out that he'd fill out the defensive back-field even if—like fifth-round picks Sherman and Chancellor—there was little in his background to indicate what was to come. He'd washed out with the Denver Broncos after having left Oregon State a year early. Looking for any way to stay in football, he then headed to the CFL.

Two or three years after that, a 6'4" muscled-up Browner made perfect sense for a corner in Carroll's defense. But at the time, he looked miscast and out of place. He didn't appear to be fast, was knock-kneed, and it looked like there were three feet between his ankles and his knees.

But, boy, did he have a nasty streak.

In 2012 after Browner had already established himself, having made the Pro Bowl in 2011, the circus that was Terrell Owens came to town. Seattle had taken a flyer on the future Hall of Famer to see if he had anything left in the tank. On the day of his first practice, you couldn't find a parking spot within a mile of the practice field because of all the media and fans who wanted to get a look at T.O. in a Seahawks uniform.

When it was time for 1-on-1 drills with the receivers and the defensive backs, everyone was watching. When it was T.O.'s turn, Browner shoved his way to the front of the line. Owens tried to stutter step to get a clean release, and Browner, who had lined up in press, man-to-man defense, locked up his shoulder pads with his oversized hands and slammed T.O. to the turf. I was too far away to hear whether Browner said anything to Owens, but I imagined a thought bubble above Browner's head that said, "Welcome to Seattle, bitch!"

Owens wouldn't stay around long, and his most memorable play came when he dropped a likely touchdown pass from Matt Flynn in a preseason game. That same year Browner knocked Green Bay Packers receiver Greg Jennings off his feet away from the ball. When Jennings got up and rushed Browner, the cornerback picked him up and slammed him to the ground again. Somehow he got away with off-setting penalties because Jennings threw a punch at him. Browner very unremorsefully flexed his arms above his head after the flags had been thrown.

In the 2011 preseason, it appeared that Marcus Trufant and Kelly Jennings or Walter Thurmond would be the starters at corner, but Browner had won the job when the season opened.

Maybe his most memorable play in the beginning of that season was a pass interference penalty in Week 2 against the Pittsburgh Steelers. On the fifth play of the game, Browner was beaten badly off the ball, and Steelers receiver Mike Wallace was an easy throw and catch from a 60-yard touchdown. Browner trailed him but got close enough to stretch that 6'4" frame out and tackle him for an obvious pass interference penalty at the Seahawks 1-yard line. Four plays later, Earl Thomas tackled Rashard Mendenhall for no gain in one of the best goal-line stands in Seahawks history and a glimpse into how good this defense could be.

Three games later Browner made a play indicative of what the Legion of Boom was all about. The Seahawks had a four-point lead in New York against the Giants, but quarterback Eli Manning had his team down to the Seahawks 10-yard line with 1:25 left in the game. A Manning pass that was intended for wideout Victor Cruz was tipped by Chancellor and picked off by Browner. He sprinted away from the entire Giants offense for a 94-yard pick-6. The game was sealed a few minutes later thanks to an interception by Chancellor. Three of the four

Richard Sherman reacts during a victory against the New York Giants in 2011, the year the Legion of Boom b
on the scene.

members of the Legion of Boom had an interception that day (Browner, Chancellor, and Thomas) and they were one week away from the fourth joining them in Cleveland.

The win in New York seemed invigorating to the team, but by kickoff the next week in Cleveland, there were three significant scratches—center Max Unger, Tarvaris Jackson, and Marshawn Lynch. To make things worse, Thurmond was injured just before halftime. Enter Sherman, the fourth member of the L.O.B.

Seattle lost the game 6–3, but Sherman filled in just fine. And in that most inauspicious setting—and before a fanbase that hardly could have really understood what was happening—the Legion of Boom was born.

Sherm got his first official start the next week against the Cincinnati Bengals and broke in his left cornerback position with an interception. A fifth-round pick who had played mostly receiver in college and had to overcome an ACL injury along the way, he finished his rookie season with four interceptions, 17 passes defensed, and 55 tackles.

One of the subplots that was brewing at that time was the emergence of what would become one of the best rivalries in the NFL between the Seahawks and the San Francisco 49ers. After all, Seattle was fairly new to the NFC West, relocating to the division in 2002 after having been in the AFC since 1977. It took a little while for some real rivalries to emerge in the NFC West. The St. Louis Rams and the last vestiges of the Greatest Show on Turf gave Seattle fits for a few years, beating the Seahawks three times in 2004 to knock Seattle out of the playoffs. But as the Seahawks then became a Super Bowl team in 2005, it seemed like no one in the NFC West was really all that good, and there weren't heated rivalries like there had been with the Oakland Raiders and Broncos, in particular, in the glory days of the Kingdome.

That began to change in Carroll's first few years with the Seahawks as Seattle rose at the same time as the 49ers did under Jim Harbaugh. The two teams were built similarly. They both wanted to play great defense and they both wanted to run the ball. At the heart of it was the Carroll-Harbaugh coaching matchup.

The two had been rivals in the Pac-10, where Carroll coached at USC, and Harbaugh coached at Stanford. There were some significant games between the two, including one of the biggest point-spread upsets in college football (and gambling) history. Harbaugh's Cardinal were 40-point underdogs to Carroll's Trojans, and then-wide receiver Sherman caught a pass on fourth and 20 that helped Stanford complete an upset at the Los Angeles Memorial Coliseum in 2007.

Two years later in 2009, Stanford had a 48–21 lead late in the game and went for two, famously prompting Carroll to ask Harbaugh after the 55–21 loss, "What's your deal?"

Harbaugh very maturely responded, "What's *your* deal?"

Harbaugh and his coaching staff were always a little chippy. Early in the 2011 season, Harbaugh's first with the 49ers, he shook Detroit Lions coach Jim Schwartz's hand after the game and followed it up with a weird, way-too-hard slap on the back that enraged Schwartz.

The first Carroll-Harbaugh battle as NFL coaches wasn't much to write about—a 33–17 win for the 49ers in the regular season opener. It was an ugly game, in which the 49ers scored all those points despite gaining just 209 yards, breaking the game open late thanks to a punt and a kickoff return for a touchdown.

Although you would've hardly known at that point the rivalry that was to come, their next meeting that season made it clear. On Christmas Eve a playoff-bound 49ers team barely emerged with a physical 19–17 win, after which offensive coordinator Greg Roman left the Seahawks press box and screamed out his best Christmas tidings: "Merry fucking Christmas!"

The 49ers hadn't allowed a 100-yard rusher all season, giving up only 77 rush yards per game. Harbaugh perfectly melded a supremely talented group of players into a very stout and talented defense. But that day the Seahawks broke the 49ers' streak as Lynch rushed for 107 yards. The Seahawks matched their 7–9 record from 2010, while the 49ers won the NFC West, went 13–3, and made it to the NFC Championship Game. But a rivalry had been born. And for the Seahawks, a corner was about to be turned.

CHAPTER 8
2012 AND THE RISE OF RUSSELL

It may be only in retrospect that you look at Pete Carroll's first two seasons and see all the signs of what was to come. As the Seahawks opened the 2012 season—Carroll's third—it was hard to know where things were really headed. Sure, the defense was showing signs of being one of the best in the league. And Marshawn Lynch was a true force. But the San Francisco 49ers seemed dominant in the NFC West, and even the Arizona Cardinals had finished ahead of Seattle in the standings in 2011.

And did the Seahawks have a quarterback? The team had sent a lot of confusing signals in the offseason, first signing Matt Flynn—regarded as maybe the best, young quarterback on the market—then spending a third-round pick on a quarterback that didn't even stand 6' tall. There was a bit of a subtext to Seattle's signing of Flynn to a three-year, $26 million deal with $10 million guaranteed. In 2011 NFC West foe Arizona Cardinals had signed Kevin Kolb from the Philadelphia Eagles, where he was a backup quarterback. He had thrown for more than 700 yards and four touchdowns during a two-game streak in 2009 and more than 1,000 yards and six touchdowns during a four-game streak in 2010. It was considered a stroke of genius at the time.

Back then, there had been a lot of hysteria from Seahawks fans, who were high on the idea of the team signing Kolb after the last two years of Hurt Hasselbeck, Mr. .500 T-Jack, and Clipboard Jesus. They finally got what they wanted in March of 2012 when they felt that the team followed the Kolb model by signing Flynn, who had been with the Green Bay Packers. He was a reliable backup to Aaron Rodgers the year before and threw for 480 yards and six touchdowns against the Detroit Lions in the last game of the Packers' 2011 season. When Seattle signed Flynn, they had gotten their Kolb.

But then there was the Seahawks' 2012 draft. In the days after the draft, the Seahawks were given a D or an F grade by multiple draft analysts. Five years later, it was seen by many as one of the best drafts in NFL history and certainly the best draft in Seahawks history.

Bruce Irvin, the first rounder, was an unknown from West Virginia who virtually no one had projected in the first round. Bobby Wagner, the second rounder, was a smallish linebacker from a small school (Utah State) who had missed the Scouting Combine because of illness. And Russell Wilson, the third rounder, was a short quarterback from Wisconsin who had transferred from North Carolina State the year before. "He'll have a Seneca Wallace-type career where you can bring him off the bench and he'll add a spark," said famed ESPN draft guru Mel Kiper Jr. about Seattle's third-round pick, Wilson, comparing him to another former Seattle quarterback.

Other significant draft choices were cornerback Jeremy Lane, running back Robert Turbin, and J.R. Sweezy, a defensive lineman the Seahawks had planned to turn into an offensive lineman. To go along with that, John Schneider had gotten Earl Thomas, Russell Okung, and Kam Chancellor in 2010. In 2011 it was K.J. Wright, Richard Sherman, and Doug Baldwin. Schneider was hitting grand slams, and no one knew it yet.

Myself and Tony Ventrella—a longtime Seattle TV sports broadcaster by then working alongside me to help cover the draft—were the first media members in Seattle to interview Wilson. From that Seahawks. com interview, it was clear that he was a great communicator. The soon-to-be rookie interviewed like a seasoned veteran. He said all the right things and even had some well-placed clichés. But as impressive as he sounded on draft day, there were few—other than the coaches and scouts inside the building—who really thought Wilson would win the three-way battle for quarterback.

Flynn seemed to be the favorite going into camp, and the team was certainly paying him like he'd be the starter. But what was obvious during interviews with the players during training camp was that the team favorite was Tarvaris Jackson. In the first preseason game, Flynn played pretty well against the Tennessee Titans, going 11-for-13 for 71 yards. Wilson, though, was 12-of-16 for 124 yards and a touchdown. Many on the outside may not have expected it, but the performance seemed to confirm the growing excitement about his play from coaches in training camp. What set him apart was that he was also the leading rusher, which included a perfectly executed naked bootleg. Wilson faked the handoff to the running back to the strong side like a magician and ran around the weak-side end for a 32-yard touchdown that fooled almost everyone in the stadium.

The next game his success continued in Denver, though officially Flynn was still the starter against the Broncos. The next week against the Kansas City Chiefs in the third preseason game was where it really all began. Going into that game, Flynn was suffering from shoulder pain that seemed suspect. He was fighting for his football life and yet he chose to not play when a rookie was on the verge of beating him out.

In that game Wilson ran for 58 and threw for 185 yards and two touchdowns. But the drive that stood out was just before the half—an 80-yard march during which he took two brutal hits from Chiefs linebacker Tamba Hali. Both were 15-yard, roughing-the-passer penalties. When he got down in the red zone, he was hit by Hali a third time but stood tall (all 5'9" of him) and delivered an 11-yard touchdown strike. At that moment it became clear: the Seahawks had a new quarterback.

Because I called that game on radio with Steve Raible, I was on the team plane. As I boarded the plane, there sat Pete Carroll in the front row with a big grin on his face. "What did you think about that?" He asked me excitedly.

I responded: "*That* was fucking awesome, Pete!"

As impressive as Wilson was in the preseason, the reality is that the regular season speeds up a bit for rookies like Wilson, especially at quarterback. Also, opposing defenses gameplan more than they do in the preseason. And the Seahawks faced a few tough teams early.

After four games Wilson and the offense were averaging a little more than 17 points and still finding their way. But Wagner, Irvin, and the Legion of Boom were allowing just 14.5 points per game and keeping the team in it at 2–2 while their rookie quarterback still had the training wheels on. Also, Tom Cable's philosophy and Lynch's Beast Mode style of running were paying off. The Seahawks averaged

150 yards per game during that period. Lynch averaged 105 per game, and the other 45 were typically filled in by rookie running back Robert Turbin and Wilson.

The Seahawks then became the talk of the NFL for their role in one of the strangest endings to a game in NFL history. The game log showed that the Seahawks beat the Packers 14–12 on *Monday Night Football*. But the story was that the game was refereed by replacement refs because of a labor dispute between the NFL and the NFL Referees Association that had surprisingly lingered into the regular season.

Trailing Green Bay 12–7 and with time for one final play as the clock ticked down to zero, Wilson looked for an open receiver, couldn't find one, scrambled out to his left, and flicked a pass effortlessly about 48 yards into the end zone where Golden Tate and Green Bay defender M.D. Jennings each leapt for the ball in a crowd. In the immediate moment as the pile came down to earth, no one really knew what happened. One official signaled touchdown; another signaled incomplete pass. Some have maintained the other official was trying to signal that time had run out. Either way, it was one big clusterfuck. In the end Tate was ruled to have caught the game-winning touchdown. Now, you *might* say that my defensive bias is at work, but I'm sorry, folks, on any other field and on any other day, that was an interception by Jennings. Long story short, the referee strike ended two days later, the Seahawks got a W, and the NFL got their referees back.

But after losing to the St. Louis Rams in the fourth game of the year, fans were calling for Wilson's head as he threw three interceptions and zero touchdowns in a 19–13 defeat. But Carroll stood behind his quarterback, and it would start to pay off. After the loss to the Rams, the Seahawks went to face the Carolina Panthers, a game that upon review was as pivotal to that season—and maybe the careers of Wilson and Carroll—as any other.

Early in the game, the Seahawks offense produced very little but led 6–3 at halftime. The first two drives of the second half, Wilson threw two interceptions. Panthers cornerback Captain Munnerlyn took one of them back for a pick-6. But again the defense kept them in the game with two key fumble recoveries. Working on that side of the ball were two rookies from that poorly graded 2012 draft. Irvin had a strip sack of Cam Newton to seal the game along with another sack, and Wagner had a four-yard sack in which he looked like he was shot out of a cannon. When I think about the emergence of Wagner's career, I think about that sack.

The next week the Seahawks came home at 3–2 to prove they were for real against another typically strong New England Patriots team— and in what remains the only time Tom Brady has played a game in Seattle. But for most of the day, a young Seahawks team seemed exposed, trailing 23–10 in the fourth quarter. Then while the defense shut down Brady, Wilson put together two straight touchdown drives. One ended with a touchdown throw on fourth down, and the other was a 46-yard bomb to Sidney Rice for the 24–23 win.

During the game Sherman decided to take on Brady. They were jawing back and forth all game. Sherman and Thomas had both picked off Brady, and after the game, Sherman went over to let Brady hear about it. Audio caught him saying, "You mad, bro?" It became an Internet sensation (with Sherman helping fuel that fire with a few social media posts of his own).

There was something more to it. Sherman's brashness oddly appealed to Seahawks fans. Fans were tired of being the nice guys and the team that almost made it and liked that Sherman talked the talk and then backed it up. Sherman was a player who thrived on conflict and, if there wasn't any, he was going to create it.

After the season Bleacher Report sent him to the streets of New Orleans, the site of the Super Bowl, to ask fans what they thought of Sherman. People's responses were: "He's fat and slow!" "He's on Adderall!" "He should keep his mouth shut!" After their comments Sherm would gladly introduce himself to them and laugh about it. At one point he was in a smack talk showdown with Skip Bayless during which he said on national television, "I'm better at life than you." His

ell Wilson prepares to throw against the New England Patriots in 2012. His fourth-quarter comeback in
24–23 victory proved he had the mettle to lead the Seahawks going forward.

bravado and bold talk struck a chord with people in Seattle. It's a modest town that doesn't scream and yell at their 2–14 team, throw batteries, or boo Santa Claus. Yet Sherman seemed to be a guy who voiced their frustration of having been ignored by the East Coast bias of the NFL.

The win against the Patriots was a big deal for Wilson and the Seahawks. Wilson had shown he could make clutch throws when it mattered most, and the defense was proving able to shut down the best of the best. But the Seahawks were still somewhat meandering. Six weeks after that Patriots game, they took their 6–4 record to Miami to play the Dolphins.

Late in the fourth quarter with a 14–7 lead, the Dolphins drove to the Seahawks' 7-yard line when Wagner picked off a Ryan Tannehill pass in the end zone. It appeared to be Wagner's second interception of the game. Thomas had rushed the throw by jumping up with his arms extended in front of Tannehill, who was scrambling out to his right. But when Thomas' hands came down, one of them grazed Tannehill's helmet, and he was called for roughing the passer, nullifying the interception. The Dolphins scored on the next play. It was a ridiculous call that could have and should have been a no call. They lost 24–21 and chalked it up to bad luck.

But there was more bad luck to come. By the time the team charter landed at Sea-Tac Airport, there was news that two players—Sherman and Brandon Browner—had been tested positive for PEDs. Seattle was 6–5, headed to another tough road trip in Chicago, and looking at two major suspensions. The season suddenly seemed like another one headed nowhere.

Browner decided to serve his four-game suspension, starting in Week 14, so he could be available for the playoffs. Sherman decided he was going to fight it, which certainly wasn't a surprise. Sherman had a problem with the collection method, and I agreed. I was randomly tested only once in my career. At the time I was spending my offseason in Scottsdale, Arizona. So they tracked me down, and I was notified that I was going to be tested, and the next day some guy showed up at my house, followed me into my bathroom, and watched me pee into a cup. He took the sample and was off to God knows where. At the time I didn't have a problem with it, but maybe I should have.

Today's players certainly should. Suspensions these days are typically four weeks with no pay. There are players today making as much as $20 million per year. A four-game suspension would cost that player $5 million. That pee tester had better show up with armed guards and a Brinks truck to protect that specimen. What they get instead is some guy who shows up in a Members Only jacket and drives off in a Ford Taurus. That's way too unofficial when that much money is on the line. There are too many mistakes that can be made, and that was Sherman's point. Sherman was vindicated and didn't miss a snap that year.

There was not a good feeling going in to play the Bears in Chicago. But Wilson's spirit came through. He had to win that game twice because his defense let the team down. Wilson put them ahead 17–14 with 32 seconds left in the game, but somehow the defense allowed a 56-yard pass connection between Jay Cutler and Brandon Marshall, getting them close enough for a Robbie Gould field goal with three seconds left and tie it at 17. So Wilson did it again in overtime with a 13-yard pass to Rice for the win. The team, including skeptical veterans like Chris Clemons, embraced Russell from that point forward. They celebrated with him, and after the game, Clemons referred to Wilson as "a baaaaad man."

This was important for the team and felt like a turning point. The Seahawks not only won, but they also overcame adversity while doing so. They also embraced their rookie quarterback as one of them. It was tough for Wilson in the beginning. He can be kind of a boy scout. It was rumored that he would come into the passing game meetings with notes and ideas for some of the veteran receivers. Veterans don't like suggestions from rookies. But now they were playing together and on the verge of something special.

Revived from a win that had saved their season, the Seahawks then beat the Cardinals so badly that they were accused of being bullies who ran up the score. The beauty of what turned into a 58–0 win—still the most points the Seahawks have ever scored—was that Wilson only threw for one touchdown. Sherman returned an interception for a touchdown, they ran for four touchdowns, and Malcolm Smith recovered a muffed punt for a touchdown.

That started an amazing three-game roll that convinced any remaining pessimist that the Seahawks were for real and made Seattle—and all of the state of Washington—feel free to fall in love with the team again. They rolled over Arizona, the Buffalo Bills, and even blew out the 49ers, scoring 150 points in three games, an NFL record. The most impressive win in that streak was the 42–13 drubbing of the 49ers. There were some revenge factors in that win for Chancellor and Sherman.

Early in the game, Chancellor tattooed 49ers tight end Vernon Davis on the 2-yard line with a hit so hard that the rest of the league felt it. He dislodged the ball from Davis' hands on a play that would've put them at the 2-yard line. He did exactly what he was supposed to do. It was a great football play. But he was penalized for unnecessary roughness, giving the 49ers first and goal at the Seattle 10-yard line. Again, it was part of the NFL's campaign to make an inherently unsafe game safe. It was a case of necessary roughness. Had Chancellor not hit him that hard, Davis would've caught the pass.

Chancellor's revenge came when the 49ers were kept out of the end zone on that drive and forced to attempt a field goal. But defensive tackle Red Bryant put his 25-pound hand up and blocked the kick, and Sherman scooped it up and returned it 90 yards for a touchdown, giving Seattle a 21–0 lead, sending CenturyLink into delirium, and handing a defeat to a 49ers team that would go on to the Super Bowl.

Sherman's revenge was not just the 90-yard touchdown. He also picked off a Colin Kaepernick pass in the end zone, thwarting his old Stanford coach Jim Harbaugh's team.

Stories had emerged that Harbaugh did not think that Sherman was an NFL-caliber player and told NFL scouts and coaches as much. So it's no wonder Sherm tended to shine in those 49ers games. There was something much bigger to come in his battle with the Harbaugh-led 49ers.

The Seahawks won their last five games that season, beating the Rams on the final Sunday to complete a late surge that had some saying they were playing as well as any team in the league. But the 49ers held on to win the division, and that sent Seattle to Washington, D.C., to play in a wild-card game against the Redskins and Robert Griffin III, who had won the Heisman Trophy the year before.

Griffin had been the second pick in the draft and ended up as the Rookie of the Year, appearing to be—along with Andrew Luck, who had been the first pick—the next big thing in the NFL. When Griffin threw a pair of touchdowns in the first quarter to give Washington a 14–0 lead, the storyline seemed to be coming to life: Wilson was good, but Griffin was the true star.

The Seahawks simply looked outmatched. But then things began to turn—not just in the game but for each team's future. The Redskins offense that year was top five in both yardage and scoring, but the Seahawks defense held them to just 60 yards and zero points in the second half.

And as they did, Wilson and the Seattle offense came to life, rallying the Seahawks for a 24–14 win that sent them to Atlanta for a divisional playoff game against the Falcons.

The one negative after only the second road playoff win in team history was that the Seahawks lost Clemons to a knee injury. Clemons was a key part to the Seahawks defense that year, holding down the Leo (weak-side defensive end) spot and recording 11.5 sacks (four in one half in the Fail Mary win against the Packers). Washington's field is notorious for having more potholes than a street in Manhattan. Had he played on any other field, he would've been okay. The breakaway turf also cost the Redskins their quarterback when RG III was sacked and stepped awkwardly, dislodging a huge chunk of grass and injuring his knee.

The Seahawks would feel the absence of Clemons in Atlanta, but I thought that game also was a showcase for tight end Zach Miller, a player who was quietly heroic that season. He'd been a Pro Bowler when he was signed as a free agent by Schneider in 2011 from the Oakland Raiders. He may have been the best blocking tight end in the NFL, a huge key to a Seattle running game that in 2012 was as effective as any in the league. But in Atlanta that day, he was a go-to guy for Wilson, catching eight passes for 142 yards and a touchdown, though even those lofty numbers don't really tell the story.

On the third play of the game, Miller tore the plantar fascia tendon in his foot. He briefly exited the game, and it was rumored that he asked the doctors and trainers to inject the bottom of his foot with painkillers. I had my ribs injected before a preseason game because I was battling for a starting spot. It is not comfortable. But having needles shoved into the bottom of your foot is a whole new level of discomfort. Miller did it and returned before the first quarter was over.

The Seahawks trailed 20–0 at the half, but they had moved the ball impressively with more than 200 yards in the first half. The problem is that they were just 1-of-5 on third downs and 0-of-2 in the red zone. At that point it seemed like a sputtering ending to a season that had generated so much hope. But as they had done the previous week in Washington, they again came back from a double-digit deficit on the road in a playoff game.

The Seahawks scored three touchdowns to take a 28–27 lead with 31 seconds left.

After all that had happened that year—signing Flynn, the much-criticized pick of Wilson, the PED suspensions, and the misery when the team was 6–5—was Seattle really going to be a game away from the Super Bowl? Before Seahawks fans could really ponder the thought, two quick Matt Ryan completions led to a Matt Bryant field goal and one of the most heartbreaking defeats in team history, a 30–28 loss. A week later the 49ers team, who Seattle had just routed, went to Atlanta and beat the Falcons to go to the Super Bowl instead.

But as the bitterness of the defeat began to wear off, everyone realized that the youth and the playmakers acquired over the previous three years also meant there was a lot of hope. Having a daily drive-time radio show, I'm able to feel the pulse of the fans as they text and call into the show. Usually after a playoff game loss, people are engaged for just a few days, pointing out blame for the loss, divvying up the credit for the good year, and eulogizing the team for that season. But this felt different. Fans felt that hope, and it continued well into the offseason. Our most hilarious and best caller told a tale of him ripping his big screen television off of the wall and spiking it on the floor when the Falcons kicked their game-winning field goal. That's a Seahawks fan for you. But the reality was that team was just a few key players away.

CHAPTER 9
2013 SEASON

There's never quite been an offseason for the Seahawks and their fans like the one leading into 2013. Sure, there was the disappointment over what might have been from the Atlanta Falcons game, especially seeing two teams Seattle had beaten during the previous two seasons (the Baltimore Ravens and the San Francisco 49ers) playing in the Super Bowl.

But this was a young team on the rise, and the Seahawks had maybe the most advantageous salary cap situation in the NFL because they had a lot of players on their rookie contracts who were elite talents yet still playing for relative peanuts. That allowed the Seahawks to make a few big moves in the offseason that on paper made the team only that much better—and heightened the excitement that much more.

It wasn't just Seattle fans who knew how good the Seahawks might be. They were also the favorites in Las Vegas to win the Super Bowl. It was a rare feeling for the Seahawks. The worry was that, as the Seahawks had done every other season in their existence—and as had all but one of the other big three major sports teams in town—that they'd come up short. But in the summer of 2013, anything and everything seemed possible.

Whereas John Schneider made some key draft choices in the previous three years that set the foundation, the 2013 offseason was about free-agent signings and trades designed to get Seattle over the top. That started in early March with a trade for receiver Percy Harvin of the Minnesota Vikings. The Seahawks sent their first-round choice (25th overall), their seventh-round pick, and a mid-round 2014 pick to Minnesota for the talented and controversial Harvin. Harvin had some baggage that included sideline arguments with coaches and a migraine headache history, but he was considered the most explosive offensive player in the league. He had a unique skillset that allowed him to also scare opponents as a kickoff returner and even as a running back, but he tended to be inconsistent.

The Seahawks followed that up with the signing of defensive lineman Michael Bennett, who was coming off two great seasons, including a nine-sack performance in 2012 with the Tampa Bay Buccaneers. He signed a one-year, $5 million deal, and I was probably more excited than most when the move was announced. In 2009 Bennett was a rookie free agent signed by the Seahawks out of Texas A&M. I scratched my head when head coach Jim Mora and general manager Tim Ruskell released him before the regular season. During that preseason he recorded two sacks for 15 yards, five tackles-for-loss, and five quarterback hits. As a pregame and postgame radio analyst that year, I named him game MVP twice in four games. So obviously I thought getting him back for $5 million was a steal.

Next came Cliff Avril, a defensive end known for his explosive pass rush, something that the loss to Atlanta had made clear that the Seahawks could use a little bit more of. He was a little more expensive than Bennett. He had turned down a long-term deal with the Detroit Lions and was coming off of a franchise tag year. There was word that he was a malcontent because of his refusal to re-sign in Detroit, but Seahawks fans would find over the years that nothing could be further from the truth. And the additions of Bennett and Avril would ultimately go down as two of the best moves the Seahawks made, putting the finishing touches on a defense about to have one of the best seasons in recent NFL history.

The 2013 draft turned out to be one of Schneider and Pete Carroll's worst, but it didn't seem to matter. The pick that maybe turned out the best was tight end Luke Willson. The fifth rounder out of Rice was fast, had good hands, and was a fan and media favorite. He didn't take himself too seriously and always had a funny quote. But the rest of the draft (see: Michael, Christine) petered out within two or three years.

Meanwhile, Richard Sherman was out there talking the talk. After his contentious appearance with Skip Bayless, I remember feeling uncomfortable about it. It was kind of an old-school thing for me about humility and the notion of doing the talking with your pads. Schneider agreed. When asked about it, he responded, "Yeah, that wasn't real impressive." But the callers and texters that weigh in on my radio show were with Sherman. They felt like he was putting the Seahawks on the map, and it was sort of an us-against-the-world mentality that they liked.

Additionally, there was distrust that the NFL cared much about West Coast teams because those teams had so many early starts (1:00 PM EST). The Seahawks had gone 1–4 in those games (including the playoffs) in 2012. The players and the fans took this as a chip on their shoulders, and Sherman seemed to represent their rebellious feelings.

During training camp that year, there was a sign that this defense was going to be special. The 7-on-7 drill, a staple of every team's practices, which pits the offensive skill players against the back seven of the defense, is structured for the offense to win. Since there are no defensive or offensive linemen involved, there's no pass rush, no offensive line to throw over, and no tipped passes for the quarterback, who can sit back there, pat the ball, and pick apart the defense. But when the Legion of Boom was on the field for those sessions, the defense was winning—something I had never seen before. Not just winning, they were dominating. Between tipped passes, interceptions, and leaving no open receivers—they were shutting Wilson's offense down. The Seahawks would need every bit of their defensive prowess to get off to the kind of start they needed to make all the Super Bowl dreams come true.

Seattle opened the season at the Carolina Panthers, a team that was developing into a good—if unlikely—rival. Much like the San Francisco 49ers rivalry, it was because they were built similarly. Both had a top 10 defense captained by a dominant middle linebacker (Bobby Wagner and Luke Kuechly). Both had a quarterback who could run and throw (Russell Wilson and Cam Newton). The Seahawks win in Carolina the year before left the Panthers with a bad taste in their mouths because Newton had thrown a fourth-down pass in the dirt on the Seahawks 1-yard line. Seattle would win again 12–7 in a game that went down to the final minutes. Three things happened in that game that were significant.

- The Seahawks won on the road in the 10:00 AM PST time slot, something that had been a vexing issue for Seattle for some time. (Carroll had intentionally started more training camp practices that year at 10:00 AM to try to get the players more used to playing that early, something the team continues to this day.)

- Wilson proved he could take over a game and win it. The Carolina defense held the Seahawks run game to just 70 yards, so offensive coordinator Darrell Bevell took off the training wheels, and Wilson threw for over 300 yards for the first time in his career in a regular-season game.
- Jermaine Kearse caught the only touchdown pass on a tightly contested go route, and over the years we would find that Kearse was like the Dos Equis most interesting man in the world. Kearse didn't catch a lot of passes, but when he did, they were epic.

It wasn't just the first game that showed the Seahawks might be up to the task of handling high expectations. This was a team that looked to be serious about everything they did, which included going 4–0 in the preseason. Everyone knows that can be a curse. The 2008 Detroit Lions went 4–0 in the preseason and then 0–16 in the regular season. But then the Seahawks started the regular season 4–0 for the first time in franchise history.

That included a win at the Houston Texans in the early time slot, a win that would become a signature victory of that season. The Seahawks kicked a field goal on their first drive of the game and wouldn't score a touchdown until the fourth quarter. Houston, which had been a good team the year before and had high hopes of its own in 2013, jumped out to a 20–3 halftime lead because Seattle's best defensive players were making mistakes—running around blocks, blowing coverages, and missing tackles.

The comeback started with a fumbled snap on their own 3-yard line, but on third and 7 from their own 5-yard line, Wilson connected with Doug Baldwin, who made a beautiful toe-tap catch that was originally called incomplete. The 98-yard drive ended with a Marshawn Lynch touchdown. With the Seahawks trailing 20–13, the Texans were close to being able to run out the clock when they ran a bootleg pass that Sherman picked off and returned 58 yards for the tie.

He ran 53 of those yards without his left shoe. At Seahawks headquarters there is a 30-foot tall picture of that play, and you can see Sherm's shoe starting to come off of his foot. We found out later that the Seahawks defense had practiced against that play all week, and every time they did, Sherman intercepted the pass. The Seahawks won in overtime with a Stephen Hauschka field goal.

It felt like that win took a lot out of them when they finally lost the next week at the Indianapolis Colts. Although they would win each of the next seven games, there were some close calls. In a *Monday Night Football* game at St. Louis against the Rams, the defense allowed 200 yards rushing, and the game came down to the defense mounting a goal-line stand because the defense allowed Kellen Clemens to drive 89 yards to the 1-yard line. Linebacker Heath Farwell, who was a special teams demon that year, made a key stop on a third-down running play to force the Rams to throw it incomplete on the final play.

The hero of the game was Golden Tate, who caught the only two touchdowns in the game and accounted for 93 of the 135 yards generated on offense. One of his touchdowns was a deep pass that Wilson threw up for grabs, and Tate turned into an 80-yard touchdown along the Rams' sideline. It was an ill-advised throw, but Tate cut in front of the cornerback and picked the floating ball out of the air. Instead of putting his head down and sprinting away from the remaining safety who was pursuing him from the middle of the field on his way into the end zone, he turned toward the safety and wagged his finger at him, which resulted in him receiving a 15-yard unsportsmanlike penalty and gave the safety enough time to shove him so hard at the 1-yard line that he stumbled into the wall in the back of the end zone. It was a play that in a lot of ways encapsulated everything about the Seahawks that season—they were the best team in the NFL and they made no apologies for putting it in everyone's face.

After a short week, the Seahawks struggled against 0–7 Tampa Bay at CenturyLink and spotted the Bucs 21 points early on. They were fortunate to get a Kearse touchdown just before the half to make it 21–7. The defense was suspect again and gave up more than 200 yards rushing for the second week in a row. But this team's ability to come back in a game and win was uncanny and a situation that Wilson thrived in. Whether it's the positivity from Carroll and Wilson (neither of them has seemingly ever had a bad day), the challenge, or their mantra that you win the game in the fourth quarter, it was working. Carroll and Wilson would continue to win in the fourth quarter and overtime for years to come. They beat the Bucs 27–24 for their second overtime comeback win and third fourth-quarter comeback win that year.

When the 9–2 New Orleans Saints came to town for a *Monday Night Football* showdown—a game that many viewed nationally as a test of just how good the Seahawks really were—there was a lot of hand-wringing over how the Seahawks would cover tight end Jimmy Graham and running back Darren Sproles. Quarterback Drew Brees had his offense putting up 400 yards and 26 points per game. What the Seahawks defense did was simple and impressive. They played a lot of man-to-man coverage. If that meant linebacker K.J. Wright or safety Kam Chancellor had to bump out and cover Sproles in motion, leaving either Wagner or Earl Thomas to cover Graham, then so be it. And they did. That potent offense produced just 188 yards and seven points. Meanwhile, the Seahawks offense put up 429 yards and 34 points.

* * *

Percy Harvin provided perhaps the most interesting drama that season. It started from Day One as Harvin showed up at the beginning of training camp with a bad hip that ended up limiting him to just one regular-season game—against his former team, the Minnesota Vikings in Week 11 (a coincidence, I'm sure). He announced he was having surgery via Twitter before the team apparently even knew about it.

You'd think there would've been more outrage over that. After all, they traded away a first-round pick and signed him to a $67-million-dollar contract with a $12 million signing bonus. But the team was doing so well that he was hardly missed. There was the thought: *Just think how good they'll be when they get Harvin back.*

In that game against Minnesota—a win that got Seattle to 10–1 heading into its bye week—he played in just 16 plays. But he did so much. He ran decoy routes that allowed other receivers to get open, he blocked downfield in the running game, he caught a 17-yard pass, and he even returned a kickoff for 58 yards. But there was more to it than just that. In that one game, you could see the effect he had on opponents. Because he returned that kickoff for 58 yards, the Vikings tried to pooch kick the next kickoff, giving the Seahawks excellent field position at their own 35-yard line. His willingness to block in the running game was impressive and unselfish, and when we talked to offensive line coach Tom Cable after the game, I mentioned that he made a couple of nice blocks. Cable corrected me: he actually had five key blocks in the run game.

The 17-yard catch he made was a key reception on third and long and it kept a scoring drive alive that would enable them to break a 10–10 tie with a rushing touchdown from Marshawn Lynch. Additionally, Harvin was great with the media. I asked him about returning kickoffs at one point because there were some who thought that he shouldn't put himself at risk and instead save himself for offense. He responded with a smile on his face. "I am a football player," he said. "I'm down with everything: running, catching, blocking, returning kicks. I want it all. I am a football player, and that's football."

As well as he got along with the media, he could not get along with his teammates. He sucker-punched Golden Tate and Doug Baldwin and displayed other bizarre behavior (such as refusing to go in to two games the following year when asked). He played so little that we were all left wondering what could have been.

It was a weird year for the receiving corps as a whole. Jermaine Kearse was emerging as a star, and Sidney Rice and Harvin were back and forth on the injury list. Tate was certainly an explosive and exciting receiver and returner, but in my mind, the most consistent, reliable receiver that year was Baldwin. He had and still has one of the best releases on the line of scrimmage in the NFL. His quickness, creativity, precise route running, and catch-to-target ratio are what make him such a big part of the success of this franchise. He is one of the best undrafted players in NFL history.

The regular season ended with the Seahawks losing just three games, and their 13–3 record gave them home-field advantage throughout the playoffs. Those three losses were by a total of just 15 points, and there was some thought that they could've gone 16–0. Others, though, noted that Seattle had won three other games by a combined 11 points, including two in overtime. Teams that finish 10–6 usually go on the road and play an extra game in the playoffs.

Going 13–3 and getting home-field advantage turned out to be critical to what happened next. It was helpful to have an off week and wait for a team in the divisional playoffs—the New Orleans Saints—that Seattle had just beaten on *Monday Night Football*. The Saints got their yardage in that playoff game, putting up more than 400, but they missed two field goals, had a fumble at a key point, and were shut out in the first half. The Saints were never really a threat after the half either, and a Lynch 31-yard touchdown run with 2:48 left in the game put the Saints away in a 23–15 victory.

Notably, before the game there was a bit of a beef between the Seahawks and Saints. New Orleans tight end Jimmy Graham was warming up on the Seahawks side of the field. Bruce Irvin asked him to move, and Graham responded, "I'm Jimmy." Irvin said something like, "Who the fuck is Jimmy?" He then took the football out of Graham's hands and kicked it into the stands. That's the kind unapologetic brashness that had become Seattle's calling card.

The NFC Championship Game between the San Francisco 49ers and the Seahawks was storybook stuff that needed a storybook ending for the Seahawks. It had the Pac-10 coaching rivalry, the two young mobile quarterbacks, the two badass running backs who refused to go down, and the two stifling defenses.

> Pete Carroll vs. Jim Harbaugh
> Russell Wilson vs. Colin Kaepernick
> Marshawn Lynch vs. Frank Gore
> Bobby Wagner and K.J. Wright vs. Patrick Willis and NaVorro Bowman
> And...Richard Sherman vs. Michael Crabtree

It may be easy to forget now that the start of the game was a disaster for the Seahawks. On the first play from scrimmage, 49ers defensive end Aldon Smith strip-sacked Wilson on his own 15-yard line. San Francisco was held to a field goal, but it was clear that the 49ers' plan was to run Kaepernick all over the place. At the half the 49ers were up 10–3, and Kaepernick had run for 98 yards.

The fans got fired up early in the second half with a Beast Mode 40-yard touchdown, and the Seahawks, who trailed by four going into the fourth quarter, had the 49ers just where they wanted them. The fourth quarter, though, got sloppy. Seattle got a favor from the 49ers because of an offside penalty that allowed Wilson to take a gamble and throw at an area instead of a receiver on fourth down, and Kearse came up with another clutch catch. Because of the offside penalty, Wilson knew he had a free play. Baldwin and Kearse were running the same go route and were within five yards of each other. Baldwin turned toward Kearse while the ball was in the air and deftly got out of his way— maybe the best play he made that day.

The Seahawks could've put San Francisco away if not for a couple of botched snaps and broken plays. The Seahawks exchanged fumbles with the 49ers deep in San Francisco territory but got the ball back with a Kam Chancellor interception that resulted in a Stephen Hauschka field goal.

As the 49ers got the ball for one final drive, Seattle was up 23–17. Then everyone really got nervous. The 49ers converted a fourth and 2 from their own 30 with 2:01 left. A third-and-2 pass to Crabtree got the 49ers another first down, and another then put the ball at the Seahawks' 18 with 30 seconds left. San Francisco had two timeouts left, so the 49ers had plenty of time and the ability to use all of the field.

But Kaepernick neither waited nor played it safe. Instead, on first down he threw a pass that resulted in a play as famous as any other in Seattle sports history. It was a dart in the back of the southwest corner of the end zone intended for Crabtree that was instead tipped by Sherman into the hands of Malcolm Smith. Three kneeldowns later, Seattle was headed to its second Super Bowl.

Sherman and Crabtree had gone back and forth since each entered the league, and now it was a chance for Sherm to let Crabtree hear about it. Sherman went over to shake Crabtree's hand in an insincere way, and that drew an unsportsmanlike penalty. Once the kneeldowns took place, the realization started to sink in. Pete Carroll and John Schneider had built a team of underdogs in just three years, and now they were going to the Super Bowl!

Then came the Erin Andrews interview with Sherman shouting into the camera like a WWE wrestler. Said Sherman: "I'm the best corner in the game! When you try me with a sorry receiver like Crabtree, that's the result you're going to get. Don't you ever talk about me." When Andrews then asked who was talking about him, he said: "Crabtree. Don't you open your mouth about the best, or I'll shut it for you real quick. LOB!"

I was doing a television postgame show with Seahawks legend Mack Strong, and after watching Sherm's antics, he was annoyed. Strong was a huge part of that '05 Super Bowl team. They had as much talent on offense as this '13 team had on defense. They had two Hall of Famers in Walter Jones and Steve Hutchinson, and Strong, Shaun Alexander, and Bobby Engram will end up in the Seahawk Ring of Honor. They had a different philosophy, a quiet strength and confidence. These antics flew in the face of that, and Strong did not care for it.

But this team had to do it their own way, and out came what Seahawks fans had learned to love: brashness. They took it all the way to New York and a date on the game's biggest stage.

Much like the game itself, it was a perfect Super Bowl experience. Radio Row was in Manhattan, and for those of us in the Seattle media, it was an elevator ride away from the lobby of our hotel. It was amazing the things the NFL paid for—a media party at one of the piers, including dozens of food trucks, bands, dancing, and even a bowling alley. During the day there was a mini-spa for the media, including wet shaves, massages, etc.

It was especially fun for me because the Denver Broncos, my other former team, were the reps from the AFC. I got to visit with former teammates like Shannon Sharpe and Terrell Davis on the radio. I went on a few Denver radio stations, and their questions were typically characterized as: "How do you think you're going to stop this offense?" The 2013 Broncos offense was one of the most prolific offenses in NFL history. They averaged around 450 yards a game and 38 points—still the highest scoring offense in NFL history. I got some funny looks when I answered their questions with, "Yeah, but you gotta see this defense."

Honestly, I wasn't sure the Seahawks could stop Peyton Manning and that Broncos offense, but I felt that there were too many special things that happened that year for the Seahawks to not win the game.

To say the Broncos got off to a bad start was an understatement. The Seahawks won the coin toss and elected to put their bread and butter on the field first. Hauschka was obviously full of adrenaline and kicked the opening kickoff eight yards deep in the end zone. Broncos returner Trindon Holliday unwisely decided to bring it out and he was swarmed by Derrick Coleman, Heath Farwell, and Jeremy Lane at the 14-yard line (maybe one of the most underrated plays of the day, considering what happened next).

On the first play of the game, I noticed that there were a lot of Seahawks fans there, and the noise advantage was real. They say that the Super Bowl crowd is typically corporate, but a lot of Seahawks fans had made their way east for this game. When Lynch carried the ball, you could hear the low grind of the "Beast" chant. When the Broncos had the ball, the Seahawks fans went to work.

Following the short opening kickoff return, Manning was lined up in shotgun and was trying to shout audibles to his offensive line. When he stepped forward so they could hear him, the center snapped the ball, and it whizzed past Manning's helmet and out the back of the end zone for a safety. Cliff Avril got credit for the points, just 12 seconds into the game, which remains the quickest any team has ever scored in a Super Bowl.

The Seahawks took the free kick that followed the safety down to the Broncos' 13-yard line and kicked a field goal. They had this 5–0 lead in part because of a Harvin 30-yard fly sweep. Once again, Harvin was making his reps count.

The third offensive play for the Broncos may have been the most significant play in the game. Wide receiver Demaryius Thomas, a big-bodied, 6'3", 225-pound receiver, ran a shallow crossing route. Waiting for him was Kam Chancellor, who belted him with a force that you imagined could almost be felt by the millions watching on TV. Thomas exploded off of Chancellor's pads and sailed five yards backward. That hit meant much more than a tackle for a two-yard gain. It sent a clear message to the Broncos: we're going to bully you.

Wilson had some nerves going on early. He overthrew a wide open Zach Miller and threw a pass to Tate in the dirt. But he calmed down, and his receivers started making plays. You could argue that late in that game Tate, Baldwin, and Harvin all could've been the game's MVP. By halftime the score was 22–0, and Manning had been picked off twice—once by Chancellor and the other time by Malcolm Smith, who returned the Avril tipped pass for a 69-yard touchdown. The game was sealed by the opening second-half kickoff when Harvin returned the kick 87 yards for a touchdown, making it 29–0.

I did the halftime update for the Seahawks radio broadcast, and by the time I left the booth, Harvin had put the nail in the coffin. On the way back to my seat, I passed one of the Denver radio broadcasters who had spent a good 10 minutes on the air, trying to convince me that the Seahawks were outmatched. We made eye contact, and he immediately averted his eyes. I thought, *Was that shame, surprise, or contempt?*

The booth that they put us broadcasters in was a makeshift box that had been built so recently that you could smell the fresh plywood and paint. There were four or five of us, all former players, shoved into a few folding chairs, watching the game through newly installed plexiglass. In the booth next to us were the Seahawks scouts, and every time the Seahawks made a play, there were high-fives and pounding fists of joy on the plexiglass. In front of us in the stands were a group of Broncos fans, and when they saw us before the game in our Seahawks garb, they were pointing and talking lots of shit. The scouts were very professional about it and ignored them. With the game in hand in the second half, the scouts ditched the professionalism and let the Broncos fans hear about it. It was hilarious to watch.

I shared a moment of reflection with Strong in that booth after everyone was gone off to do radio, and he and I were getting ready to go down and do television on the field. Strong wasn't bitter that this team had won it all and his team hadn't. Instead he started talking about Super Bowl XL and how there was too much complaining about the refs. He said that had they put that energy into the game, they might be feeling the way this team did. It was a poignant moment, and as bad as I felt for having never sniffed a Super Bowl in my nine years in the league, I felt worse for Strong, who was so close.

Everything about that trip was magical. There were no glitches during the week other than Harvin punching Tate in the eye the night before the game, though you'd never have known it the way the team played the next day, which spoke loudly to what kind of team that was. The game could not have been more fun. Once the kickoff took place, the game was never in doubt.

For the after-party, Macklemore played until 4:00 AM, and Carroll was up on stage. A brutal snowstorm hit, but it didn't start to stick

sell Wilson raises the Vince Lombardi Trophy after helping guide the Seahawks to a 43–8 victory against Denver Broncos in Super Bowl XLVIII.

until every team charter was in the air and headed back to Seattle. It was destined to be the Seahawks' Super Bowl.

I was at CenturyLink where the Super Bowl parade ended. It was wild. It was freezing cold, and I remember Lynch pounding on some kind of Native American drum and drinking Fireball. He headed out of the tunnel with a champagne bottle when head equipment manager Erik Kennedy wrestled it away from him. That was about the only thing the Seahawks lost all season.

CHAPTER 10
2014 SEASON

If there had never been an offseason of anticipation like the one the Seahawks and their fans felt going into the 2013 season, then there had never been an offseason of celebration like the one they all experienced in 2014. It seemed like the party continued all offseason—even after the game and the parade. There was the visit to the White House, the presentation of the rings, the debut of the official Super Bowl highlight film at a downtown Seattle theater. It was a rare offseason that no one may have wanted to end.

But the business of the NFL also meant some quick and harsh realities. The Seahawks had benefitted from one of the most favorable salary cap situations in the NFL the previous few years. It was a young team of players with many playing on team-friendly deals. But that began to change in 2014 as the Seahawks had to pay some of their top players. Things never stay the same in sports or life, but things never would be quite the same for Seattle as they had been in 2013.

It was difficult to part ways with players like Red Bryant, Chris Clemons, Brandon Browner, Breno Giacomini, and Walter Thurmond, who were all key parts of the run to the Super Bowl but would never again play for the Seahawks in a regular-season game, following that night in New Jersey.

But it was especially tough when Golden Tate was signed by the Detroit Lions, and the Seahawks didn't match. Those players were expensive and they had to clear cap space to re-sign the likes of Richard Sherman and Earl Thomas, but they were enjoying the luxury of not having to pay their quarterback just yet. It's a winning formula when you have great young players operating on the rookie minimum salaries. When those players came due, it was a whole different situation.

In the meantime, because of the last collective bargaining agreement that limited players to a slot in their first four years, third-round pick Russell Wilson was a steal. He led his team to the divisional round of the playoffs as a rookie in 2012 and a Super Bowl championship in 2013, threw for more than 6,400 yards and 52 touchdowns, and ran for more than 1,000 yards and five touchdowns, and the Seahawks were paying him in the hundreds of thousands instead of the tens of millions.

Despite the personnel losses and some change in the team, most of the key parts returned, and Seattle was still regarded as the favorite to win the Super Bowl in 2014. And the Seahawks looked ready to repeat when they blew out the Green Bay Packers on a Thursday night in a season opener. It was as festive a night as Seattle could ever have. The national media was focused on the Seahawks, live bands played before the game, and they unveiled the Super Bowl banner.

It was also the one night when it looked like the Percy Harvin trade just might work.

Harvin amassed 100 yards of offense (41 rushing, 59 receiving), and the way that offensive coordinator Darrell Bevell used him on the fly sweep was seen as revolutionary. It's amazing to me, though, when NFL analysts introduce offensive schemes like that as "revolutionary." I coached the defense for Interlake High School here in the Seattle area in 2007, and every time we played Liberty High School, a school in our conference, we had to deal with the fly sweep. It was a concept that high school and college coaches had used for years.

My high school coach, the great Joe Sellers, used an offense known as the single wing back in the early 1980s at Wooster High School. It had the same principles of the wildcat that was used in the NFL by the Miami Dolphins in 2008. The reality is: for all the names people want to put on plays and all the schematic breakdowns we see after every game from "experts," there are only so many things you can do on offense.

To put it simply, the fly sweep is a reverse, in which a receiver goes in motion, and the quarterback times the snap perfectly so he can hand the ball off to a speedy player like Harvin running full speed. If he gets to the corner of the defense, he can gain as much as 30 yards, as Harvin did in Super Bowl XLVIII. Harvin ran like a deer and was made to play football physically. But football tests you in every way as a person. It tests your mental, emotional, and physical toughness. It can make you feel like you're on top of the world one moment and not worth a damn the next—especially at the professional level. There are men who are more athletic and better players than the best players in the NFL, but if they don't have the discipline and mental toughness needed, they're worthless.

A Seahawks teammate of mine, linebacker Sam Merriman, told me that his high school linebacking crew of four included himself and two other linebackers who were also playing in the NFL. I asked about the fourth linebacker, and he told me two things: he was by far the most talented player of them all and he was in prison. There is so much more than just talent that goes into making a good football player.

A Week 2 loss to the San Diego Chargers was quickly righted with a win the following week in a Super Bowl rematch against the Denver Broncos, as well as a victory at the Washington Redskins. That gave Seattle a 3–1 record, going into a game against the Dallas Cowboys.

Up until that point, Harvin had as many chances as anyone to make plays, fit in, and win games. To Bevell and Pete Carroll, he was like a shiny new toy. They couldn't wait to use him. He ran the fly sweep, caught screen passes, and even lined up as a running back. The point was to get him in space where he made things happen. Against the Chargers in the second game of the year, he was the leading rusher. All of his yards came on one play. He was lined up in the I-formation behind Marshawn Lynch at fullback. All 10 players went to the right, but Harvin sprinted to his left, Wilson flipped the ball to him, and he outraced the entire Chargers defense 51 yards for a touchdown.

Harvin was fun to watch. I'm not sure how fast he ran the 40-yard dash, but he was one of those players who played faster than his speed. Although he was just 5'11" and 185 pounds, I was told that he was "crazy strong." There was a rumor that in *another* fight during Harvin's time in Seattle, he picked up defensive lineman Tony McDaniel and tossed him to the side to get to another player. McDaniel was 6'7" and weighed 300 pounds.

One other forgotten fact that may have set Harvin off was that in Week 4 in that *Monday Night Football* game against the Redskins,

Harvin scored three touchdowns that were all called back because of penalty. He scored on a 22-yard fly sweep (holding on James Carpenter), a 26-yard receiver screen (false start Harvin), and a 41-yard pass down the middle of the field (unnecessary roughness by Carpenter). Whatever the reason, Harvin wasn't happy, and that day against Dallas, he did something I've never seen in all my days as a player and an analyst—he refused to go into a game. It was perplexing. In that game against Dallas, he was the second most targeted receiver and had been the *most* targeted receiver in two of the first three games. In other words, he was getting his opportunities.

Carroll is seen as a new age, progressive coach who is player-friendly. But Carroll also has his limits and is more old school than people think. His No. 1 rule is: protect the team. Harvin certainly wasn't doing that, having turned down an opportunity to help his team. It didn't help that this occurred in a game they lost to Dallas 30–23.

Harvin was gone five days later. In the end the $67 million player, who the Seahawks had traded a first-round draft choice for, was traded to the New York Jets for a conditional draft pick. I wish I could've unscrewed Ben Obomanu's head and put it on Harvin's body.

Obomanu went to Selma High School in Selma, Alabama, and was valedictorian his senior year. He attended Auburn and would later get his law degree from the University of Alabama. Obo was a seventh-round selection of the Seahawks in 2006 and spent his rookie year on the practice squad. Every year after that, he was one of those guys on the bubble at the end of training camp, who was teetering on the cut list. Yet between 2007 and 2012, he always made the team because he was a decent receiver, a really good special teams player, and an excellent human being and teammate.

The Harvin trade and a loss to the St. Louis Rams two days later had some around the NFL beginning to debate if the Seahawks were going to be a one-hit wonder. *Sports Illustrated* put the Seahawks on the cover with a headline stating, "Heavy Lies the Crown."

But in the loss to the Rams, Wilson exploded and made everyone forget about Harvin. He threw for more than 300 yards and ran for more than 100 yards, making him the first player to do so in NFL history. But the Seahawks also had dropped to 3–3 and were facing another long road trip to play the Carolina Panthers in a 10:00 AM start.

It turned out to be a game just like the last two trips to Carolina—a low-scoring slugfest that would put the Seahawks on a late-season roll. The game ended on back-to-back sacks of Cam Newton by Bruce Irvin, and the Seahawks got out of there with a 13–9 win. In Irvin's third year, he was certainly playing like the first-round draft choice he was in 2012. He had two interceptions for touchdowns that year: a 35-yard, pick-6 against the Oakland Raiders and a 49-yard, pick-6 against the Rams in the last game of the regular season.

Irvin's versatility was phenomenal. He had played safety in junior college and was a hand-in-the-dirt pass rusher at West Virginia. The Seahawks had him play some linebacker, and his instinctive pass coverage was surprisingly superior and the very thing that allowed him to make those plays. A pick-6 for a defensive player was a dream come true, but Irvin couldn't care less about those plays. He told us on our show that he would gladly turn those plays in for sacks. Along with the two interceptions for touchdowns, he recorded 6.5 sacks that year—not enough for him, he would tell you.

After the win at Carolina, Seattle almost ran the table—a loss to the Chiefs in Kansas City in below-freezing temperatures was their only defeat in their final 10 games. Something that had reared its ugly head was run defense. It came up in the Houston, Tampa, and St. Louis games the year before and was the reason they lost to both Dallas and K.C. in 2014. As good as they were defensively at just about everything, they looked bad when run gap integrity got sloppy.

The pass defense was another story. Because of the added pass rush from Irvin, Michael Bennett, and Cliff Avril and the Legion of Boom, the Seahawks defense had only given up one 300-yard passer in two years, and that was Drew Brees in the divisional playoff game the year before. They held Brees to 34 yards passing in the first half of that game when it really mattered, and the rest came in garbage time when the game was in hand. In the 38 games they played in 2013 and 2014 (playoffs included), they allowed less than 200 yards passing in 23 games, a phenomenal feat.

Their other strength was something Carroll preaches every day—"it's all about the ball." Other than point differential (obviously), the turnover ratio (takeaways minus giveaways) is the most indicative statistic in the NFL. If you're in the top 10 in turnover ratio, it gets you 10 wins on average and into the playoffs 80 percent of the time. When all was said and done, the Seahawks collected 63 takeaways in 2013–14, and 41 of them came on interceptions. The offense did their part as well, giving the ball away just 33 times those two years or less than once per game.

High on the list of memorable plays that year was the Beast Quake II run by Lynch to spark a blowout win against the Cardinals in Arizona. First of all, it was an eerily similar play to the original Beast Quake run. It also had a pulling right guard, a number of broken tackles, Lynch throwing a defender (Rashaad Johnson in this case) to the ground with his free hand, and a crotch grab when he leapt over the goal line 79 yards later.

On the first Beast Quake, Matt Hasselbeck ended up catching up in time to help Lynch celebrate in the end zone. Against Arizona it was Ricardo Lockette, who accompanied Lynch down the sidelines and into the end zone. Lynch had been ill early in the Arizona game, but it was the Cardinals he made sick with his run that helped clinch a big win.

The play also led to one of Lynch's famous press conferences. Lynch might have been able to escape the media, but a small visitor's locker room meant a few reporters were waiting when the doors opened. He decided to have some fun for the minute or so that he talked, greeting every question with the answer of: "Thanks for asking." There was no one like him.

* * *

For the first time in the Pete Carroll era, the Carolina Panthers had to come to Seattle. This first-round playoff game was a rematch of the critical mid-season win. All of the usual suspects showed up in this game. Russell Wilson was a 68 percent passer with three touchdowns and no interceptions. The other Willson (Luke) had four catches and a touchdown. (He always seemed to play well against Carolina.) Doug Baldwin caught a touchdown, and big-play Jermaine Kearse had a spectacular 63-yard touchdown, in which he held off the defender with one hand and caught the ball with the other hand and sprinted to the corner of the end zone where he dove for the score. Richard Sherman picked off a pass and had a chance for a second one. Earl Thomas broke up two passes and led the team with 11 tackles.

But it was Kam Chancellor's game. The stats show he had 10 tackles, but that hardly said all of it. He also hurdled over the line twice in a row to attempt to block back-to-back field-goal tries on the final play of the second quarter. It was spectacular to watch. Although he didn't block the first attempt, the Panthers had an illegal motion penalty. On their second attempt, he hurdled the line again, forcing a bad kick, but he ran into the kicker. The third try was good by Panthers kicker Graham Gano to cut the lead to 14–10 at halftime, but psychologically it had an effect on the Panthers. They felt like, *What do we have to do to score?*

Then came the coup de grace. To ice the game for good, he jumped a stop route and picked off a Cam Newton throw for a 90-yard touchdown with just under six minutes left in the game. The Seahawks were headed back to the NFC Championship Game, which would prove to be even more difficult than the year before.

So many things had to go right for the Seahawks in the second half against the Green Bay Packers. I remember thinking, *Hey, it's been a good run. Maybe they can get back to Super Bowl next year.*

The Packers led at the half 16–0, and it felt worse than that. It just sort of felt like it was not going to be Seattle's day. Certainly, Wilson could not have had a worse first-half performance. He was 2-of-9 for 12 yards and three interceptions. On one of the interceptions that he threw, he was rocked by Packers linebacker Clay Matthews on the run back. It was a hit that would've given 99.9 percent of people on this Earth a severe concussion. But Wilson was unfazed.

The Seahawks didn't score a point until five minutes left in the third quarter and had to rely on their punter Jon Ryan throwing a pass to an eligible offensive tackle (Garry Gilliam) on a fake field-goal attempt. That cut the lead to 16–7.

But any hope that would immediately turn the game Seattle's way didn't really happen, and when Wilson threw his fourth pass intended for Kearse, resulting in his fourth interception of the day, with 5:13 left in the game and the Seahawks trailing 19–7, it felt over. But Morgan Burnett, who had intercepted the pass, slid down on his own power at the Seattle 46-yard line with at least 20 yards of room to run. That might've been enough to set up the Packers for a field-goal attempt. (He appeared to stop after seeing teammate Julius Peppers directing him to do so.)

It can be argued he did the safe thing so as not to fumble the ball back to the Seahawks. But it may have cost the Packers that game. The Seahawks defense did their job tackling Packers running back Eddie Lacy for -2, -4, and a two-yard gain. Then the offensive core of the team—Wilson, Willson, Marshawn Lynch, and Baldwin—went to work to get a quick score to make it 19–14. Then it was up to kicker Stephen Hauschka and the Seahawks special teams to execute an onside kick, a play that works about one out of four times. (Those odds are down to 8 percent with the new rules.)

Chris Matthews, a tall receiver from the CFL that the Seahawks activated before that game, recovered the onside kick, though there was a little more to it than that. Green Bay positioned its return team so that reliable receiver Jordy Nelson was in position to catch it on a bounce. Backup tight end Brandon Bostick was lined up in front of Nelson and was supposed to block any oncoming Seattle players. But when Bostick saw the ball, for some reason he forgot about his assignment and decided to go for the ball. It instead glanced off his pads and bounced free so that Matthews could get it. Sometimes it takes a break like that to make it to a Super Bowl.

Four plays and 44 seconds later, Lynch was in the end zone, giving Seattle a 20–19 lead. So, of course, they went for two. The two-point play was in crisis from the very beginning. It was meant to be a rollout to Wilson's right, but there was a jail break by the Green Bay defensive line, and Wilson was running for his life. He ran an S route and heaved the ball off of his back foot about 40 yards back across to the left. Willson was blocking and showed great awareness by leaking out to the left as the safety valve in case things went wrong. He double-clutched the catch but brought it in just as he crossed the goal line to give Seattle a 22–19 lead. Of course, Aaron Rodgers was going to lead his offense down the field to kick the tying field goal with 14 seconds left. And he did set up a 48-yard field goal by Mason Crosby.

Seattle won the overtime toss (thank you, Tarvaris Jackson), but Baldwin had a terrible kickoff return that only got them out to their own 13-yard line. He made up for it with two catches for 45 yards and got them down to the Green Bay 30-yard line and within Hauschka's range. A Peppers sack made it third and 8, so they took one shot to the end zone, and Wilson did the unthinkable. He threw to the guy he had targeted five times in that game—one was an incomplete pass, and the other four resulted in interceptions. When Kearse hauled in that touchdown pass, the stadium, which had been quiet for all but about five minutes of that game, erupted.

Wilson threw it to Kearse after seeing Green Bay in a Cover-0 defense, meaning no safety in the middle of the field. That was the proper call against that defense, but it also says something about Wilson's faith in his teammates that he threw it to Kearse despite all that had happened to that point. And it also says something about Kearse: he made the catch despite all that had happened all day and he did it with Tramon Williams draped all over him. Other Seattle players said later they thought it would be a touchdown the minute they saw the way the

inst the Green Bay Packers' Cover-0 defense, Jermaine Kearse catches the game-winning touchdown in NFC Championship Game.

Packers were aligned. It was the second straight year a Wilson-to-Kearse deep pass for a touchdown had helped decide a conference title game.

I was standing in the opposite corner of the stadium in an open-air mezzanine where we were to broadcast the postgame show on television. It was one of the most adrenaline-filled, exciting moments of my life. People were hugging, high-fiving, and just screaming. Wilson was in tears and couldn't talk. When asked by our sideline reporter, Jen Mueller, "What was the plan?" Baldwin shouted on live radio, "There was no fucking plan!" Michael Bennett went over and grabbed one of the Seattle Police Department bicycles and started riding around the stadium, high-fiving fans. It was the best party I had ever been to.

131

And now the Seahawks were on to Phoenix to see if they could win a second straight Super Bowl and enter the ranks of the immortal teams in the NFL.

* * *

Injuries ended up playing a huge role in Super Bowl XLIX against the New England Patriots. In the NFC Championship Game, Richard Sherman, who had picked off an Aaron Rodgers pass and played his tail off, had gotten his elbow in the one place on the field you don't want it—in between a ball carrier and Kam Chancellor. He played most of that game as a one-armed man.

Safety Earl Thomas also suffered a shoulder injury against Green Bay that would require offseason surgery, but, of course, he was going to play through that. Then in the week leading up to the Super Bowl, Chancellor hurt his knee in practice. They rushed him to the hospital, and Chancellor was in tears. He thought that there was no way he could play in the game. Ultimately, a game-time decision up until kickoff, Chancellor willed himself to play, and on gameday you couldn't tell he'd been injured.

During the game, though, two more injuries did the defense in. Late in the first quarter, defensive back Jeremy Lane picked off a Tom Brady pass in the end zone and returned it to the Seattle 14-yard line, where he was tackled by Patriots wide receiver Julian Edelman. With all of the things that happened that game, that was the turning point in my mind. Edelman hit him low in the knee, and Lane went sailing through the air. He landed awkwardly and snapped his arm in half on the turf. I spoke with a team doctor after the game, and he said very gravely, "that was a bad break." The replay was gruesome to watch.

A couple of months later, Lane was in a grocery store and felt his knee, where Edelman hit him, start to slide. He went back to the team doctor to find that he had also injured his knee, requiring surgery. Lane was a very good slot defender. Most teams these days spend a lot of time in a nickel defensive personnel grouping, in which they take a linebacker out and add an extra defensive back to the lineup so they can match up when there's an extra receiver in the game. Lane may have been the best nickel or slot defender in the league. With the injury to him, they were forced to move cornerback Byron Maxwell into the slot and put Tharold Simon on the outside at corner. Maxwell was up to the task and had played well in both spots, but Simon was getting beat, and Brady and the Patriots picked on him the rest of the game.

Then in the third quarter during a Bobby Wagner interception return, defensive end Cliff Avril got a concussion and he was out of the game as well. Seattle scored following that interception to take a 24–14 lead midway through the third quarter.

Even with all that adversity, Seattle had gotten the lead thanks in part to some gutsy play right before the half. Late in the second quarter, Russell Wilson engineered a hurry-up offense drive that got them to the New England 11-yard line with six seconds left. They had a timeout remaining, but with that little time left, there was some risk in going for it and not just kicking the field goal. Not only did they go for it, Wilson threw it to Chris Matthews, the tall CFL product who had recovered the onside kick two weeks before and had not been active the entire regular season. It was just the second pass he had thrown to Matthews, and the first one went for 45 yards earlier in the quarter. This one went for a touchdown to tie the game at the half. Matthews would finish with four catches for 109 yards and a touchdown, making him a legitimate MVP candidate for the game.

Thanks to Wagner's pick and the resulting touchdown, Seattle had a 10-point lead going into the fourth quarter, and it was easy to think a second straight Super Bowl win seemed a given, but Brady is Brady, and with the Seahawks' defense being banged up, the Patriots scored two touchdowns in the fourth quarter to retake the lead. You can imagine Pete Carroll wonders what would have happened with a healthy defense that day.

Given the way the Seahawks have so often rallied with Wilson at quarterback, though, you also had a thought that maybe this only meant that the Seahawks had them right where they wanted them—trailing by four in the fourth quarter with 2:00 left. And then Jermaine Kearse did it again.

Wilson launched a 35-yard pass down to the 5-yard line, and Kearse out-battled cornerback Malcolm Butler. The pass was tipped up in the air, and while Kearse fell to the ground, he kept the ball alive with his right knee and then his right hand and secured it with both hands while lying flat on his back. Kearse may sometimes have frustrated fans by dropping some easy ones, but he sure had a knack for making the big dramatic catches. But there was confusion after the play. The officials felt it was a catch and marked it on the 5-yard line, but the Seahawks weren't sure, and perhaps thinking the Patriots would challenge it or call a timeout, they didn't get the next play to Wilson in time and had to burn a crucial timeout.

The next play was a run, in which Marshawn Lynch looked like he was going to cross the goal line, but linebacker Dante Hightower clipped Lynch's heel, and he went down at the 1-yard line. Now the next part still makes my adrenaline surge and still makes me sick to my stomach. The Seahawks' next play was a pass on a pick play that was thrown to wide receiver Ricardo Lockette. That pass was intercepted, and the Seahawks lost 28–24.

But there was much more to that, and the decision to call that play, the lack of execution, and whose fault it was are still being picked apart in Seattle to this day. Before you just say, "Run the damn ball," there are some things you should know. In order to use all three plays they had left with only one timeout remaining, one of the plays needed to be a pass. That way if it was incomplete, it would stop the clock, they could call a running play, they could call a timeout, and they could have a chance for another running play. (This brings the timeout they had to use after the Kearse catch back into focus.)

Furthermore, the Patriots had their heavy or goal-line package in, which meant eight defensive lineman and linebackers and just three defensive backs, whereas the Seahawks had one tight end, one running back, and three receivers. There is not an offensive coordinator in the NFL who wouldn't have tried to take advantage of that. That matchup screams: "Throw the ball!"

Also, Wilson's pass was the 109th pass from the 1-yard line in 2014, and it was the first one intercepted. I'm sure the Seahawks coaching staff weren't privy to that statistic. But the fact is that kind of thing just didn't happen.

So what went wrong and why? On the side of the throw, Kearse was split out to the right about eight to 10 yards and up on the line of scrimmage. Outside of him one yard away and off the line of scrimmage was Lockette. The two defenders—cornerbacks Brandon Browner and Butler—were layered or staggered in their alignment, meaning Browner up on the line of scrimmage, and Butler was back, so they wouldn't run into each other and make a pick play easy for the offense.

Here's what they should've done: get lined up after the Kearse catch and run a play—any play—so you save your timeout. Secondly, just give the ball to Beast Mode. Thirdly, at the snap of the ball, Kearse was supposed to drive Browner off the ball so as to bump off Butler so he couldn't intercept the ball, but he didn't. The fourth point is Lockette must run hard, but he didn't. If he'd run a more aggressive route, maybe Butler doesn't make the interception. And, finally, it was a bad throw by Wilson.

Here's the fact of the matter and really all that mattered: Butler made what was maybe the best play in Super Bowl history. That he was able to run into Lockette, blow him up, and hang on to the ball is a miracle of modern physics. The one lasting image from that game emblazoned in my mind was the real-life look of horror on Richard Sherman's face as he watched that play unfold. As you might expect, the locker room was a mix of anger and shock after the game. Luke Willson has referred to it as "sad guys and mad guys." Some were crying, and some were pissed. One player shattered his right hand punching a locker. Carroll and offensive coordinator Darrell Bevell had to head to the main interview area just after the game and explain and defend the call. Lynch beat a hasty exit to the bus.

The dumbest conspiracy theory to come out of that was that Carroll and the coaches didn't want Lynch to win the MVP of the game and thought that Wilson was a better MVP, and that's why he threw in that situation. So some think that Carroll's thought process was: *Do I want to win two Super Bowls in a row and join the likes of Vince Lombardi, Don Shula, and Chuck Noll and ensure my enshrinement into the NFL Hall of Fame? I do but not if it means having Lynch as MVP. Not on my watch!* That is idiotic.

There's a saying in sports: don't let the same play beat you twice. The question to ask in the years to come is: how many times would that play beat them?

CHAPTER 11
A SUPER BOWL HANGOVER

The airing of grievances lasted about two weeks after Super Bowl XLIX. Blaming offensive coordinator Darrell Bevell for calling a pass play was the most popular complaint. Then it was Jermaine Kearse for his inability to drive Brandon Browner off the ball, even though they never would've gotten in that game or been in that position without Kearse's spectacular play. Ricardo Lockette should've turned defensive back and knocked the ball out of Malcolm Butler's hands. Even Russell Wilson was blamed.

Then, no one wanted to talk about football. The plummeting ratings for sports radio in Seattle were indicative of how Seahawks nation felt about football following the shocking loss to the New England Patriots. National media, though, continued to put a spotlight on the game. Some called the play call among the worst in sports history and the defeat as heartbreaking as any in sports history. But Pete Carroll said the Seahawks would move on, saying in one interview the defeat would not define him or the team. So the Seahawks pretty quickly got back to the business of football.

Like the year before, there were some major losses to free agency, but that's what happens when you make back-to-back Super Bowl appearances. Following the 2014 season and the near-miss against the Patriots, the Seahawks also made a couple of major acquisitions. Having other teams come poach your players via free agency is also what you get when you have a legendary defense.

In 2014 the Seahawks defense firmly marked itself as one of the best in the history of the game: the defense allowed 528 fewer yards than the next closest team. They were top five in nearly every category and allowed no more than 15 points per game in the past three years. That offseason two of the more underrated players and two of my favorite players flew the coop

Linebacker Malcolm Smith was a seventh-round choice out of USC in John Schneider's second draft in 2011. I always felt that he was a starter in the NFL, but K.J. Wright and Bobby Wagner were among the best linebackers in the league, and because defenses spend about two-thirds of the time in nickel (five defensive backs and two linebackers), he didn't spend much time on the field. But when he did get on the field, he was always around the ball. He had two touchdowns, including the one in Super Bowl XLVIII that made him MVP. That same year he caught the famous tip in the NFC Championship Game. But following the second Super Bowl, he signed a big free-agent deal with the Oakland Raiders, getting the kind of big payday Seattle couldn't give him.

I always felt that if Richard Sherman wasn't in town, we would've been raving about Byron Maxwell. He was physical, was rarely beaten deep, and made plays on the ball. Maxie had some of the best punch-out forced fumbles outside of Chicago, where the Bears' Charles "Peanut" Tillman perfected the move. It was fun to watch because "punch out" is typically a term in football when someone forces a fumble, but like Tillman, Maxwell would literally make a fist to punch the ball out of the ball carrier's arms. There was no way, though, that the Seahawks could keep him following the 2014 season. Maxwell scored a huge contract with the Philadelphia Eagles that included $25 million guaranteed. As much as everyone hated to see him go, all were happy for Maxie.

To compensate for the loss of Maxwell, the Seahawks made what in some ways was almost like a trade with the Eagles, signing veteran Philadelphia cornerback Cary Williams. It was a signing that came with mixed reviews and even more mixed results. He just wasn't a valid fourth member of the Legion of Boom.

Late in the season, a safety-turned-corner named DeShawn Shead took over for Williams. Not only did he replace Williams in the starting lineup, but the Seahawks also cut Williams after he played in just 10 games despite having signed him to a three-year contract that included $7 million guaranteed. The signing seemed to further teach the Seahawks a lesson, as Williams served as the second talented corner that they signed from another team who didn't work out. In 2013 they signed Antoine Winfield, who had recently been a Pro Bowl corner for the Minnesota Vikings. He was cut before the team's run to a Super Bowl title even began.

Shead, who took over at corner that year, was a rookie free-agent safety in 2012 out of Portland State. He was a decathlete in college and a tremendous athlete but appeared to be more of a good special teams player and a very average safety. When they moved him to corner, I thought it would be a mistake, but Shead flourished. It seemed that home-grown corners worked much better in this defense, and players like Maxwell and Shead were home grown.

The biggest move that offseason, though, was the trade for New Orleans Saints tight Jimmy Graham, who was in a contract battle with the Saints, and the gist of the battle was that he wanted to be categorized and paid like a receiver instead of as a tight end. Tight ends made about $8 million, and receivers made about $12 million. Since his relationship with the Saints had soured, and the Seahawks were willing to trade their first rounder and Max Unger to the Saints *and* pay the final three years of a contract, paying him $10 million a season—the most for a tight end in the NFL—the Seahawks were able to get Graham.

This was a move that made sense because the Seahawks offense lacked a red-zone threat. Now, you should know that I have a tendency to think that every problem can be solved with Doug Baldwin. It's about getting a clean release and separation from the defender, and there was no one better at that than Baldwin. But they wanted a big-bodied target for Wilson (particularly after what happened at the end of the Super Bowl), and Graham was 6'7", a former college basketball player at Miami, and averaged 10 touchdowns per year in New Orleans. At the end of his three years in Seattle, no one was sure whether it was worth it.

One of the pitfalls in going to the Super Bowl in back-to-back years is having your players signed away by other teams. The other is the divvying up of credit. Who are the most important players? Who are the players that helped you the most to get to the Super Bowl?

Well, Kam Chancellor felt he was one of them, and I can't say that I disagreed with him. Chancellor was the soul of that defense and that team. He always had a smile on his face (except when he was hammering an opponent) and had a quiet style of leadership that was beloved by all. But he felt a little underappreciated so he held out of training camp and—to the surprise of just about everyone—ended up missing the first two games.

Dion Bailey, a free-agent safety from USC, played well in camp and the preseason, and, though everybody loved Chancellor, people were pulling for Bailey. The situation also provided a glimpse into an interesting fan/player/team dynamic. Chancellor was as popular with fans as any other player. His hit on Vernon Davis in 2012 is still cited by a lot of fans as one of their favorite Seahawks moments ever. But as loyal as fans are to individual players, they will always side with the team in these situations. They side with the billionaires (team owners) and not the millionaires (the players).

Where I think that comes from is that your average fan probably played football or is married to someone who played football, and it sinks in with them that pro football players are ultimately getting paid to play a game for a living. It's worse if the player is not honoring a contract, as was the case with Chancellor. I must admit that the older I get, the more I side with the owners and the more intolerant I am of players who complain about a piece of paper that has their signature on it. Chancellor gave no interviews to anyone while he was holding out, which made it all that much more mysterious. And then after the holdout was over, he wouldn't talk about it anymore.

What also made the holdout a little mysterious is that Chancellor had two years remaining on his contract, and the Seahawks had set a precedent of not wanting to give extensions to players who had more than a year remaining and drew a line in the sand with Chancellor. But to many fans, it was mostly about the money, and Chancellor had an average salary of more than $7 million a season. I do side with the players when fans make comments like, "I'd play for a lot less than that." My response to that has always been "Yeah, I'm sure you would, but no one would pay to come see you play because you suck!"

The Chancellor holdout made for a weird and rough beginning to the 2015 season, one in which Seattle already faced long odds in trying to get back to the Super Bowl for a third straight year, something only two teams—the 1971–73 Miami Dolphins and 1990–93 Buffalo Bills—had done to that point. They have since been joined by the Patriots.

The Seahawks also had a tough place to start the season—in St. Louis against the Rams, where Seattle had lost two of the previous three years. With under a minute left in the game and down 31–24, the Rams split their tight end Lance Kendricks out wide, knowing that Chancellor's backup would follow him and cover him man-to-man. As Bailey turned to run with the go route, he stumbled, and Kendricks scored, tying the game, which led to an overtime loss for the Seahawks.

The next week Bailey got just nine snaps, and the Seahawks dropped to 0–2 after losing in Green Bay to the Packers 27–17. After that Chancellor ended his eight-week holdout despite not getting another dime from the team. And when he returned, he said all the right things. "I've always been a guy who follows my heart, and just watching my teammates and my team play week to week—first, second game—watching those losses, it hurt me, being the leader that I am," he said. "It was very hard because, not taking away from anybody else, but I knew I could make a difference."

After the holdout he was at every practice, every camp, always helping the younger players. He was the epitome of a team guy, as he was before the holdout. This had the rubber band effect on how fans and teammates felt about Chancellor. Fans and teammates loved him even more. First of all, it was clear that they really did need Chancellor because they were 0–2 without him. Secondly, the Seahawks won the next two games *with* him and actually won because of him when he forced a fumble at the end of the Detroit Lions game. Also, after a holdout like that, it's difficult for a player to walk back inside the locker room with his tail between his legs. NFL players are tough competitors, and I imagine it was tough for Chancellor to swallow his pride and admit defeat.

The Seahawks held their ground and sent a message that they would not be held hostage over a contract dispute, no matter how important the player. There was nothing official, but the Seahawks

r holding out the first two games of the 2015 season, Kam Chancellor excitedly comes out of the tunnel ng his return to action against the Chicago Bears on September 27.

indicated that they "worked" with Chancellor on some of the fines that were imposed during that period.

* * *

Jimmy Graham did not seem to be the panacea that the Seahawks thought he would be for their offense, especially down inside the red zone. He had just two touchdowns, and it wasn't until Week 11 vs. the Pittsburgh Steelers that they used him correctly, in my opinion. He was covered man-to-man several times that year, especially inside the red zone. I felt that getting him the ball there should be a priority. Throw up a jump ball to him any time that happens. The most clear case of that came in the Steelers game, and Graham came down with a 36-yard catch on the 1-yard line. They split him out to the left, and he had only the corner to beat, and Russell Wilson put up the perfect jump-ball throw. But later in the game, he tore his patellar tendon and was done for the year.

The low point of that season came just after the bye week when they suffered a 39–32 home loss to the Arizona Cardinals. That left the Seahawks at 4–5. The season had not gone how anyone had planned, but the team's goals were still in reach if it could make the kind of second-half turnaround it had made in 2014 (and basically every other season under Pete Carroll). Seattle has always turned it on in November and December since he arrived in 2010.

Every player spends his time off during the bye week differently. As a player I tried to get away but never too far. There is a certain amount of misery that you dedicate yourself to when you enter the season in training camp. I never wanted to even sample anything that felt like the offseason during the season. Wilson thought about it differently

Because of my philosophy, I was taken aback by what came from the Wilson/Ciara bye week. They flew to Mexico on a private plane, and on social media, there appeared what looked like romance novel cover photos. They were riding horses on the beach, dancing under palm trees, and sipping drinks through straws out of coconuts. It was strange to me but to each their own. Wilson came to camp as a rookie with a wife. Then they got divorced, and he met the musician Ciara and got married with much fanfare. Wilson frolicking on the beach in Mexico even resonated a little negatively with the fans, especially when they lost at home in his first game back. It was only the fourth time since 2012 they lost at home, and Wilson also threw an interception and completed just 44 percent of his passes.

But that was all forgotten when Wilson went on a legendary tear, which wiped out any notion that he was a game manager, only good throwing outside the pocket, or affected by his *Lifestyles of the Rich and Famous* vacation. From that point forward, the Seahawks went 6–1, and that was without Graham or Marshawn Lynch. Rookie free-agent sensation Thomas Rawls ran for 830 yards by Week 12, but then he broke his ankle. Wilson had to take over and he did.

Among his accomplishments, he had the NFL's highest quarterback rating (110.1) for the year and an eye-popping 132.8 rating during that 6–1 streak. Wilson has always been a great passer on the run but was seen as a play-action passer who relied on the running game and his mobility. He was 73 percent in the pocket that year and threw 31 touchdowns and just seven interceptions. He became the first quarterback in NFL history to throw for 4,000 yards and more than 30 touchdowns while running for more than 500 yards.

Part of the discussion that year was that Graham played in just two games of that seven-game offensive explosion. Many felt it was addition by subtraction, but that's not what I saw. I thought it could've been even better with him, but tell that to Doug Baldwin. According to Sheil Kapadia of ESPN, Wilson had an 80.4 percent completion percentage when targeting Baldwin during that stretch. According to ESPN stats, no other quarterback/wide receiver combination has posted a higher number in the last 10 years. As ESPN also noted, Baldwin became the only player in the last 15 years to post a 1,000-yard season while catching at least 80 percent of his targets. Overall, Baldwin finished with 78 catches for 1,069 yards and 14 touchdowns, the latter a team record and tied for the most in the NFL.

So yeah, the passing game was getting it done. And the Seahawks defense—even if it was mad at the offense—was still doing its thing. By the end of the season, they had allowed just 17.3 points per game, accomplishing something that not even those great Chicago Bears defenses could by allowing the fewest points in the NFL for four straight years. They had done it with three different defensive coordinators: Gus Bradley, Dan Quinn, and Kris Richard. And that brought into focus something that was clear: it was Carroll's defense.

When Carroll took over as coach in 2010, he wanted to do three things really well. Once he got the players that he wanted like Lynch, Wilson, Chancellor, Richard Sherman, Earl Thomas, etc., he accomplished all three. He wanted to play excellent defense—check. He wanted to run the ball. They had a top five running game every year from 2012 to 2016. Finally, he wanted to take the ball away on defense and take care of the ball on offense. The Seahawks were at least plus-7 in turnover ratio, including plus-20 in 2013, every year from 2012 to 2015.

Carroll came to Seattle in 2010, but it wasn't until 2012 that he got the players that he wanted. In 2010 they were integrating players from the past and churning through transactions like crazy. In 2011 they started to get players like K.J. Wright and Sherman—players that specifically fit what he wanted done on defense. Then came the 2012 draft, and Carroll had his signature players.

The Seahawks put their stifling defense on display the last game of the season. They traveled to Arizona to play the Cardinals and the best offense in the NFL that was putting up over 400 yards and 30 points per game. They chased MVP candidate Carson Palmer out of the game, as he had one touchdown, an interception, 129 yards passing, and a completion percentage below 50 percent. As much attention as the offense had brought to Seattle, the defense was still world class.

After smoking the 13–3 Arizona Cardinals, the big bad wolf in their division, by a score of 36–6, the Seahawks had a 10–6 record and reached the wild-card game in the playoffs. The hangover from the lost Super Bowl the year before had seemingly disappeared, but something before the first playoff game—a road contest against the Minnesota Vikings—was a reminder that there were still some bad feelings.

A photographer with *The Seattle Times* tweeted out that Lynch wasn't there when the Seahawks boarded the buses to fly to Minnesota. He had been hurt that year, giving way to the rookie sensation Rawls. With Rawls out, Lynch had come back into the fold after undergoing surgery on his groin midway through the season. He had practiced all week, taking the majority of the repetitions in practice. But when the buses departed for Sea-Tac Airport, Lynch was not on board. This was a surprise to everyone, including Carroll, who was informed on the bus that Lynch decided to stay behind without telling anyone.

To put it nicely, Lynch had never been the easiest player for the Seahawks organization to handle. After he held out prior to the 2014 season for about a week—with some hints that he considered retiring—the Seahawks wanted to reassure Lynch in 2015, handing him a two-year contract extension that meant he was now making more than $10 million a season. But the ending to Super Bowl XLIX left a sour taste that Lynch just could not get rid of. After Super Bowl XLIX, when the Seahawks did not give him the ball on the 1-yard line, Lynch was heard saying something to the effect of: "Fuck this. I'm outta here."

It was well-known that he felt there was some conspiracy against him—whether it was the NFL or the Seahawks—and that they didn't want him as the face of the NFL or the Seahawks. He thought they would much prefer that squeaky clean Wilson was the face. Lynch had refused to speak to the media the past two Super Bowls and was famous for the "I'm just here so I don't get fined" comment. He had stayed out on the bench during halftime of a game in freezing temperatures at Kansas City, something I had never even heard of before.

He wore a Chancellor jersey out to practice during Chancellor's holdout (something that the organization let him know afterward he shouldn't do again) and he had called the shots on his own surgery,

147

travelling to Pennsylvania to get his groin/core procedure. Lynch was a malcontent. But there had not been anything like this before.

During the week it's important to take reps in practice if you're going to play in the game. Since they had been planning to play Lynch and not Christine Michael, Lynch had taken all the reps that week. To not inform your head coach that you're missing the trip is beyond subordinate. That was the Super Bowl hangover rearing its ugly head.

To further complicate things, it was cold in Minnesota—historically cold. It ended up being the third coldest playoff game in NFL history at -6 degrees and -25 with the windchill. At the half the score was 3–0 because of a bizarre play by punter Jon Ryan. Punting from Seattle's own 25-yard line, Ryan fumbled the snap, and his timing was off. He still had time to punt the ball, but he panicked and started running, needing seven yards to get a first down. Had he just broken to his left, he had a convoy of blockers, and the Vikings players on that side of the field had turned their backs and were running down field. He broke right instead and was upended short of the first down. He landed head first, and his helmet came down on his nose, causing two black eyes that were an embarrassing reminder for about a week.

Another gaffe turned into a spectacular play that encapsulated Wilson's command on the football field. A shotgun snap took Wilson by surprise, and, though he did get a hand on it, the ball went 10 yards the wrong way. He slid down to pick it up. When he looked up and saw he still had time to get up, he sprinted hard to his right to avoid the sack and threw it across his body to the middle of the field where rookie wide receiver Tyler Lockett was wide open, and Lockett took it to the 4-yard line.

Watching Wilson on that play made me realize why he is so good in the fourth quarter and overtime. Because he wasn't expecting the snap, he was still holding his mouthpiece in his right hand. As he ran back to collect the fumbled snap, he very methodically put the mouthpiece in his mouth, secured the ball, sprung off the ground, found an open receiver, and threw the ball.

We sometimes kid in the media that Wilson is actually a robot because of his predictable answers and the fact that he never gets rattled by a question or a play on the field. That same robotic process allowed him to throw the ball to Jermaine Kearse in the NFC Championship Game, even though Kearse had four drops that led to four interceptions. So it was just like a computer program would run: put mouthpiece in— check. Secure ball first—check. If there is time to get up and throw the ball away, do so—check. Create space to make throw—check. There was no panic, and he did what he is programmed to do. Two plays later Wilson found Baldwin open for a touchdown.

When you're doing things the right way and work hard every day to get better and never take short cuts, things go your way. Teams that make it to the playoffs year after year and win Super Bowls aren't just lucky. There's an old saying: "The harder I work, the luckier I get."

This had been the case for the Seahawks since 2012...mostly. The ball bounces your way, the penalty flags go your way, and when it comes down to making or missing field goals, that goes your way, too. That was the case for the Seahawks that year. Because with just 26 seconds on the clock and an opportunity to win the game with a field goal that was inside of an extra point, Vikings kicker Blair Walsh missed a 27-yard kick and gave the Seahawks a pass to the second round of the playoffs to take on the Carolina Panthers.

The Seahawks had enjoyed playing in Carolina over the past four seasons, but it was the Panthers that had given them one of their four home losses back in Week 6. The Seahawks were down a couple of players, including Bobby Wagner back then, but now were at full strength, and Lynch actually got on the bus this time. If they won, there was a feeling that going to Arizona to play the Cardinals would be a ticket to another Super Bowl, considering how they handled them in the final game of the regular season.

But the first play of the game was indicative of how the game would go. Panthers running back Jonathan Stewart ran for 59 yards against a defense that looked slow and confused. At halftime the score was 31–0.

They fought back, and the defense held them to just 70 yards and zero points in the second half. With the help of two Jermaine Kearse touchdown catches, the offense scored 24 points. But the comeback and the onside kick, which they had famously recovered the year before, was smothered by Carolina linebacker Thomas Davis.

CHAPTER 12
2016 AND MARSHAWN MOVES ON

While my good friend and former teammate John Elway's revamped and defensively dominant Denver Broncos took apart the Carolina Panthers in Super Bowl 50, a tweet from @MoneyLynch rocked the world of Seahawks fans and briefly diverted the attention of the NFL away from the biggest game of the season. Fittingly, for a player who was as media averse as any in recent memory, it included no words. Instead, it featured only a peace sign emoji and a pair of lime green football cleats hanging over a telephone wire. There had been rumors that Marshawn Lynch might retire, and the tweet confirmed it. Still, it was a surprise and something of a shock to the system and it came before Pete Carroll, John Schneider, and Seahawks nation could really digest how they felt about him.

If most of Lynch's Seahawks career had been Hall of Fame worthy, the end had been ugly. He had chosen to skip a playoff game and ran for just 20 yards on six carries in the other.

There were mixed feelings because it was clear that his teammates loved him, but him not getting on the plane to go for the Minnesota Vikings game was pretty close to Percy Harvin refusing to enter a game against the Dallas Cowboys in 2014. He had given Seahawks fans some amazing moments on the field and reflected something that is in a lot of Americans: a resistance to authority. His running back coach Sherman Smith told us on the radio, "Marshawn does not like to be told no."

Ultimately, it was Lynch sort of telling the Seahawks no—or at least, no more. He retired 10 months after the team gave him a big contract that it came to regret. But one of the few constants in professional sports is change, and it was after the 2015 season that the roster that had taken Seattle to two Super Bowls and the brink of two others really began to undergo a little facelift.

Russell Okung, who had been the first pick in Carroll and Schneider's first draft and a solid blind-side tackle for Russell Wilson, negotiated his own deal with the Broncos. Defensive tackle Brandon Mebane, who had quietly been one of the best Seahawks on or off the field in franchise history, signed with the San Diego Chargers. Mebane was productive on the field and a mentor and example to all about what it meant to be a professional. Bruce Irvin, a defender who was every bit as versatile as Kam Chancellor, Bobby Wagner, and K.J. Wright, was offered a contract with the Oakland Raiders that the Seahawks would've been crazy to match.

That was also the case with J.R. Sweezy, who signed a contract with the Tampa Bay Buccaneers that would pay him more than $6 million per year. Sweezy was a Carroll special. He was a defensive tackle at North Carolina State, and they drafted him to play offensive guard. This is something that Carroll would do successfully a number of times and perhaps more revolutionary than people may think. I had played tight end in high school and was recruited at Notre Dame as a tight end/receiver. I went to Stanford and played linebacker for four years and can't imagine what I would've thought if the Seahawks had drafted me and then asked me to play tight end in the NFL. For me it was hard enough to make it to the next level—let alone switch to a position that I had not played since high school.

But not everybody got away. They re-signed punter Jon Ryan, who had been a steady performer and was now the longest tenured Seahawks player once Mebane left. They also re-signed Jeremy Lane, whom I thought was the No. 1 priority going into free agency. It's difficult to find good cover corners, and Lane could play both in the slot and on the outside.

The most controversial signing turned out to be receiver Jermaine Kearse, who was always something of a lightning rod with Seahawks fans, who seemed to either love him or hate him. I have always been a fan of Kearse's because of the number of big catches he made over the years. He was a free agent in 2012 and was not especially big or fast, but within one year, he was making catches like the fourth-down play in the NFC Championship Game vs. the San Francisco 49ers for what turned out to be the game-winning points, the overtime game-winner against the Green Bay Packers in the NFC Championship Game the next year, the circus catch in Super Bowl XLIX, and the one-handed catch and score in the Carolina playoff game in '14. But when you mentioned his name, it seemed a lot of people were only thinking about the four targets in that Green Bay game that resulted in four interceptions and the pick play that wasn't on the 1-yard line in Super Bowl XLIX. There was not a player in Seahawks history who brought such a wide range of both praise and criticism. But in my mind, next to Wilson, Kearse is the most clutch player in franchise history.

One of the biggest keys to the Seahawks success in the Carroll/Schneider era has been the consistency—and durability—of Wilson. And while Wilson didn't miss any games in 2016, the Seahawks found out what it's like when their quarterback is even just a little less than 100 percent. One player who can do a lot of damage is defensive tackle Ndamukong Suh, and he stepped on Wilson's ankle in the 2016 season opener against the Miami Dolphins. It looked bad. Wilson was headed to the turf—face first—while his toe was in the ground. Suh stepped on his heel, and Wilson's lower leg twisted in a way it shouldn't.

Two weeks later against San Francisco, he was tackled by 49ers outside linebacker Eli Harold, and that looked even worse. I've seen and been a part of a lot of gruesome-looking knee injuries on the field. You get used to it, and having witnessed my own knee dislocated while looking down and seeing my leg stuck in a twisted mess and pointing the wrong way, I've gotten somewhat immune to it. This wasn't entirely gruesome, but in my estimation, it was definitely an injury that was going to cost him a few games—if not the entire season.

Wilson missed one play.

Maybe the most remarkable quality about Wilson—more than the comebacks, the records, and his ability to always have a positive attitude, no matter what the odds—is his ability to stay healthy. In 2013 in the overtime win in Houston, he was *blasted* along the sidelines by Texans defensive lineman J.J. Watt. Wilson just bounced up and trotted back to the huddle while Watt had a bloody nose that looked like a crime scene. On one of the four interceptions that he threw against Green Bay in the famous comeback NFC Championship Game, he was *rocked* by Packers linebacker Clay Matthews during the interception return. Matthews was flagged for an illegal blind-side hit that snapped Wilson's head in a way that usually results in a concussion.

I've seen a lot of those injuries, too, and that one looked like a concussion to me. Wilson didn't miss a snap and brought his team back for the win. So neither Watt, Matthews, nor Suh—who all would go down on just about anybody's list of the top 10 most fearsome defensive players of the past decade—could bring down Wilson, a player who was supposed to be too small to play quarterback when he entered the NFL in 2012.

That one play that Wilson missed in the 49ers game is the only play that he has ever missed because of injury. He also had to miss a play in a 2017 game at the Arizona Cardinals to have a quick neurological exam to determine if he had a concussion. To this day he has yet to miss even one repetition in practice.

Wilson and Lynch worked so well together with the zone-read offense, giving Seattle one of the best running games in the NFL every season from 2012 to 2015. Everyone knew the offense would look different in 2016 without Lynch. But with Lynch gone and Wilson at less than 100 percent, replicating those numbers proved a challenge. Schneider and Carroll still wanted to run the ball, of course, and though Lynch was gone, free agent Thomas Rawls had run well as a rookie the prior year until he was injured.

The rest of their stable of backs included Christine Michael, who had been chosen with their first pick in the 2013 draft at No. 62 overall; rookie C.J. Prosise, a third-round pick out of Notre Dame; and Alex Collins, a fifth-round pick from Arkansas. Anytime a rookie plays well, I consider it a small miracle. I realize that personal experiences can be deceiving, but that's how it went for me. I was lost my rookie year and spent most of my time worrying about screwing up or getting fired. You could say that I needed someone else's head screwed on top of my body. But for me and a lot of players in the NFL, the second year is when the game slows down, and you just go out there and make plays like you used to in high school and college.

Rawls had performed so well as a rookie—and as an undrafted one at that—that it was very rational to think he was going to be the player that kept the Seahawks running game in the top five. He got off to a slow start in the win against Miami, averaging just 2.7 yards per carry, but it looked like just a bad day for him. But the next week in Los Angeles against the Rams, he had seven carries for -7 yards, and you could see there was something wrong. He had no patience, no sense of timing, and no confidence whatsoever.

If you put his play to music, it would be to "Flight of the Bumblebee." He was all over the place while also going nowhere. In what was his best chance to fulfill all the high hopes that greeted his arrival, Michael wasn't much better. Proise showed flashes of brilliance that included a 72-yard touchdown against the Philadelphia Eagles and he went for more than 100 yards running and receiving against both the New Orleans Saints and New England Patriots that year. But in the end, the running game was very inconsistent, and they finished as the 25th best running team, averaging just under 100 yards per game. How bad was it? That season I counted more than 100 running plays that went for one yard or less.

Some players love playing professional football. Others like the idea of being a professional football player. Michael, unfortunately, was the latter. I don't mean to be harsh, but he showed so much obvious talent at times—and even some real toughness when he stepped in for Lynch in the freezing cold in Minnesota and provided just enough yardage to get the Seahawks past the Vikings in the playoffs. But for every glimpse of greatness came a behind-the-scenes step back that frustrated the Seahawks' powers that be.

Michael once missed part of a walk-through practice so he could go inside and get a hat. Another time he missed a preseason scrimmage because of illness when the starting running back job was up for grabs. Sorry, but I'm tough on that one because I played in a *Sunday Night Football* game against the Raiders with a 103-degree temperature and fluids coming out of both ends. Another time, the Seahawks intended on running a flip play to him, where the entire offense went to the right while they flipped the ball to him going left. When the snap was fumbled, he waved his hand in disgust and marched off the field instead of diving into the pile to retrieve the fumbled snap. He showed visible disgust by clapping his hands together when the Seahawks audibled out of a play (possibly tipping the fact that he wasn't going to get the ball). And in the kind of play that maybe best encapsulated the Christine Michael experience, he once nailed a rushing linebacker to the ground on a jailbreak blitz with a perfectly executed and brutal block. But he was the safety valve on that play so that Wilson could dump the ball off to him in case he got in trouble. Well, Wilson was in trouble, so instead of turning and looking for the ball, he flexed his arms while standing over the linebacker he had just crushed, and Wilson's pass hit him in the back of the head. I know how tough it is to sustain a career in the NFL, but sometimes your personality or your behavior can get in the way. I'm sure I didn't do everything the right way, but I hate to see someone with all the talent in the world not take advantage of it.

* * *

The 2016 season was as odd as any in the Pete Carroll-John Schneider era as it was hard to know what to expect from one week to the next. The Seahawks were still playing excellent defense. After four amazing years as the No. 1 scoring defense, they dropped just two notches to No. 3, allowing just 18.2 points per game and still had a positive turnover ratio by the end of the year. They proved that to the New England Patriots in a meeting that was their first since they'd come up short in Super Bowl XLIX. They traveled to New England to play in a *Sunday Night Football* game against the 7–1 Patriots as 7.5-point underdogs and having had to play the previous Monday against the Buffalo Bills.

Russell Wilson, who will always have to prove he is on the level of the best passing quarterbacks in the NFL, did just that, throwing for three touchdowns and no interceptions while Tom Brady threw one interception and no touchdowns. Wilson finished with a 124.6 quarterback rating, and Brady's was 90.1. C.J. Prosise was spectacular. He ran for 66 yards and was targeted seven times with seven catches for 87 yards. My favorite play was a catch he made along the sidelines. He could've stepped out of bounds to avoid contact. Instead, he lowered his shoulder and blasted Patriots safety Patrick Chung.

But that game was won on defense. On the first drive of the game, Brady and the Patriots set an NFL record by having thrown 252 passes without an interception to start the season. Three series later, the Legion of Boom ended that streak when DeShawn Shead picked off a deep Brady pass.

A battle between Kam Chancellor and Patriots tight end Rob Gronkowski was in the making. On the first drive of the game, Chancellor was in press coverage (on the line of scrimmage) one-on-one with Gronk and was called for pass interference in the end zone, giving the Patriots the ball on the 1-yard line. They scored the next play. Later in the second quarter, Chancellor again was up on the line challenging Gronkowski, who was split out to the right. He ran a post pattern, slightly angling into the middle of the field. Chancellor masterfully tipped the perfect throw from Brady away, and at that same moment, safety Earl Thomas hit Gronk in the middle of the chest, causing him to spend the next few plays on the sidelines.

With a little more than a minute left in the game and the Seahawks clinging to a 31–24 lead, Brady found Gronkowski for 26 yards down the left sideline. The connection gave the Patriots first and goal on the Seahawks 2-yard line and made it Brady's 75th 300-yard passing game, which was the third most in NFL history.

The Seahawks answered by putting together one of the best goal-line stands in NFL history. Once again, the Patriots split Gronkowski out. This time he was on the left, and there was Chancellor once again challenging him with one-on-one coverage. You could've argued that there was illegal contact initiated by both players, but the referees let them play, and the pass fell incomplete, and the Seahawks went home with a 31–24 win.

After that game more than a few national pundits thought that maybe we'd see yet another Seahawks-Patriots Super Bowl. Seattle looked that good that night. But with Wilson hurting for part of the season and without a good running game, they were all over the board. It was just a weird year, to say the least. The first two weeks, the offense scored just 15 points. In three games that year, they scored single-digit points, going 0–2–1 in those games, including the infamous 6–6 tie at the Arizona Cardinals.

They also suffered their first championship era "ABR" (after Bobby Wagner and Russell Wilson) with a blowout, 38–10 loss to the Green Bay Packers, a game in which Wilson threw a career-high five interceptions. Making it even more confusing was the fact that they had blown out the Carolina Panthers 40–7 the week before, though they'd also lost Thomas for the season against the Panthers, so maybe we should have known something was coming.

The special teams in that Arizona game featured the good, the bad, and the spectacular. Seahawks wide receiver Tanner McEvoy blocked a punt, kicker Stephen Hauschka missed a field goal for the win, and there was an awesome field goal block by Wagner, who timed it just as Chancellor had done two years before in the playoffs vs. Carolina, but he landed perfectly, blocked the kick, and pulled in the ball almost all in one motion.

Wagner was part of that historic draft of 2012. He was the second-round pick that year and a big question mark because he had played his college ball at Utah State—not exactly a football powerhouse. He had missed the NFL Combine because of an illness. Right after he was drafted, I was part of the Seattle media group that talked to him about it on a conference call. When asked about that, he revealed that he was throwing up and coughing up blood. I turned to the person next to me and said, "That's awesome!" That's a linebacker for you.

In Week 15 of the 2016 season, Wagner made a play against the Los Angeles Rams that showed what he was all about. On fourth and 1 at the Seahawks 7-yard line, the Rams decided to go for it, thinking that their star running back Todd Gurley would surely pick up one yard. Using perfect technique in shuffling to the outside of the tackle box and keeping the proper spatial leverage on the ball carrier while maintaining good pad level, Wagner performed as close to a perfect tackle as you can make and stopped Gurley in his tracks for no gain.

Contrary to the ferocity that Wagner plays the game with, he is a mild-mannered guy off the field who doesn't say a lot and is always professional. You might describe him as shy. In his first couple of years, he used to sport a Teenage Mutant Ninja Turtles backpack on the plane for away games. Over the years he became the kind of linebacker that I always wanted to be—a playmaker. He is always around the ball, but when it's time to do the dirty work, he fits the bill. When he hits you, you stay hit.

There are two things that NFL players openly brag about: their speed and their basketball skills. They're also reticent to give out praise to anyone else. Because of my involvement with the team broadcasts and the radio show I am on, I get a chance to talk to almost every player on the team at some point. When we ask players about who is the fastest player on the team or the best basketball player, Wagner's name comes up quite a bit.

He is a humble man and has never uttered an ill word. As I mentioned, the divvying up of credit was a problem in the years after the two Super Bowl appearances for some players. Some grew bitter whether it was about money or fame—but not Wagner.

Richard Sherman was another story. Sherman is an intelligent, logical thinker and understands the game of football as well as anyone I've ever met. As much as his emotions have a tendency to get in the way, I don't think he'd be the player that he is without being so irascible and stubborn. But if the 2011–15 seasons showed all the good in Sherman, as he became one of the best and most loved players in team history—and having made a spectacular play with his tip against the San Francisco 49ers that will always be one of Seattle's best sports moments—things unfortunately began to go a little haywire in 2016, foreshadowing the messy ending to his career in Seattle.

In Week 6 the Seahawks survived a scare against the Atlanta Falcons, narrowly winning a 26–24 game. The Falcons exploded for 21 points in the third quarter, and one of those touchdowns was a 36-yard touchdown pass to Julio Jones. After the play there were some confused looks, and Thomas put his hands up in the air as if to say: "Where were you on that?" It wasn't clear who it was directed at, but there was definitely confusion over on right side of the defense where Sherman plays. That was one of the four games Chancellor missed that season, and backup safety Kelcie McCray was in the game. Although McCray filled in nicely, there's no substituting for the communication that Sherman and Chancellor had developed over the years.

It turned into a situation on the sideline where there was a lot of screaming and yelling. If I had to guess, there was a rule that either was inconsistent or didn't make sense in Sherman's logical mind. With a defensive scheme, you need very specific rules. Otherwise you have exceptions, and the more exceptions you have, the more complicated it becomes and the more you have to commit to memory. I got the sense from Sherman's outburst that this had happened all week in practice, and now it was popping up in the game. The result was Sherman yelling and screaming very passionately at either his teammates, coaches, or both.

Although this got a lot of attention on the TV broadcast and seemed to be all anyone wanted to talk about after the game, this was not newsworthy to me. I had cursed out coaches and teammates alike and have been cursed out by them a number of times during the heat of battle. This has gone on for years in the NFL, but it has never been as closely monitored as it is today. I had a screaming match with a linebacker coach on the sidelines of a game once. When I got on the team bus, he said something to the effect of "Screw you." I said, "Screw you, too." Then we had a beer together on the plane flight home. It's just how it goes.

In fact, after someone asked offensive line coach Tom Cable, who had been standing near the defensive backs during the screaming match, about the incident, he replied, "Wait...what happened?" So it was much ado about nothing.

But nine weeks later, what Sherman did in a Thursday night game against the Rams was a little different. With a 10–3 lead late in the third quarter and a first and goal at the 1-yard line, a Wilson pass was almost picked off in the end zone. This hit a little close to home for everybody, causing all to reflect on the look of horror on Sherman's face when he witnessed the interception, also at the 1-yard line, that killed Super Bowl XLIX.

Honestly, I thought it was a bad play call, too. The Seahawks got away with one this time because that was as much of an incomplete pass as Golden Tate's "Fail Mary" was a catch. Because of the goofy catch rule at the time, Rams linebacker Bryce Hager was robbed of an interception. Either way, this set Sherman off, and he let Pete Carroll and offensive coordinator Darrell Bevell hear about it.

But after the review came back and the incomplete pass was upheld, the Seahawks did run the ball on second down, and it was stuffed for no gain. There's a very good chance that would've happened if the Seahawks had run the ball at the 1-yard line vs. the Patriots in Super Bowl XLIX because of the personnel mismatch. Then the Seahawks threw it again to a wide-open Doug Baldwin, and it, of course, worked. Throwing the ball from the 1-yard line is not a stupid idea. Baldwin juked Rams cornerback Troy Hill off the line so badly that Hill was 10 yards away from him when the ball was thrown. That is the play I would've liked to see them run in Super Bowl XLIX.

Nevertheless, instead of celebrating the touchdown catch in the end zone, Baldwin, who had witnessed Sherman's outburst over the pass play, sprinted to the sidelines and handed the ball to Carroll and Bevell. When asked about the play after the game, Sherman threw more fuel on the fire, admitting he was mad about the play call and said, "I was letting [Bevell] know…We've seen that, and I'm sure you guys have seen that play enough times."

The next week at Sherman's press conference, I was sitting in the middle of the room, and, of course, he was asked about it. All he had to do is just say: "Coach Carroll and I worked it out and we're past it." Instead he started by saying that players have a say in what play is called. I closed my notebook, got out of my chair, and left the room.

I like Sherman. We're both from Stanford. Deep down, he's a kind dude, and I admire his play as much as any player I've known. Whenever I think about a late-round draft choice who turns into a gem, I think of two players: Brady, who was taken in the sixth round, and Sherman, who was taken in the fifth. But I had had enough.

Unfortunately, the controversy was nowhere near its end. My ESPN 710 Seattle co-host, Jim Moore, asked Sherman, "What I don't quite understand is that Bevell is calling plays that he thinks will work, and yet you think you have a better handle on play calling?"

Sherman responded, "But let me guess: you have a better play to call. Let me guess: you have a better experience." When Moore said no, Sherman said, "Then you should probably stop."

The press conference ended a few minutes later. As Sherman walked off the stage and down a walkway that headed out of the auditorium, he passed Moore and said, "You don't want to go there. You do not. I'll ruin your career."

Moore replied: "You'll ruin my career? How are you going to do that?" (Jim later told me, "If anyone is going to ruin my career, it'll be me." Moore wanted no part of it and didn't want or need an apology from Sherman.)

Said Sherman: "I'll make sure you don't get your media pass anymore."

Sherman pretty quickly took to Twitter to apologize, but he then announced he would not speak to local reporters for the rest of the season. And though he softened a bit on that, he just seemed grouchy the rest of the year—just another sign of how much things had changed since that glorious night in New Jersey. But Sherman's hard-headedness and confrontational demeanor probably helped him become the kind of player he was.

* * *

Good fortune when it comes to a team's injuries or lack thereof is way more important than calls going your way and balls bouncing your way. In the Carolina Panthers game, Earl Thomas collided with Kam Chancellor, and Thomas broke his leg. The next week they were blown out and allowed 38 points to the Green Bay Packers, featuring a play that you would never see with Thomas roaming in the secondary—a 66-yard touchdown pass. Thomas' backup was Steven Terrell, and sadly he just didn't belong in the Legion of Boom.

Barely minutes after he was injured and before the game had even hit halftime, Thomas tweeted that "a lot is running through my mind, including retirement." It was bizarre, but something that we came to expect later on. Thomas is a different cat. He's hard to follow and sometimes says things that you wouldn't expect. More often than not, after an interview with Thomas, I wanted to say, "What do you mean, Earl?" The defense was not the same without Thomas, and the question of who is the most important player in the Legion of Boom was answered.

With all the turmoil in that year, it was amazing that the Seahawks went 10–5–1, won the NFC West, and had a home game in the playoffs. But they caught a little bit of a break when the Detroit Lions, who were riding a three-game losing streak, came to town for the wild-card game, and the Seahawks dominated them pretty quickly. It felt like a win from 2013. They held Matt Stafford to a 75 quarterback rating and Detroit to just two field goals. On offense, Russell Wilson scored a 119 quarterback rating, throwing two touchdowns and completing 77 percent of his throws.

Wilson's performance was expected. Doug Baldwin's performance—104 receiving yards and a touchdown—was expected. But Thomas Rawls' performance was a surprise. He ran for 161 yards. He was his old self and offered a glimpse into what he could be if he just turned his brain off and played football. Sadly, we'd never see that again—either in that season or in Rawls' NFL career with the Seahawks.

In Atlanta the following week for the divisional playoff game against the Falcons, things started out promising. After a holding penalty on the kickoff, Wilson put together a 14-play, 89-yard drive that took eight-and-a-half minutes off the clock. Against an Atlanta offense that was as prolific that season as any in the history of the NFL, that was exactly what Seattle would need to do to win the game.

But in the second quarter, it all started to unravel. What appeared to be a 52-yard touchdown to Paul Richardson was ruled a 33-yard catch that was down by contact. They were then held to a field goal. A lot of Seahawks fans, myself included, forget that the Seahawks rented returner Devin Hester for that postseason. It appeared that he was going to pay off right away. He fielded a punt at his own 13-yard line and returned it 80 yards to the Atlanta 7-yard line. But there was a holding penalty on the play, taking the Seahawks back to their own 7-yard line. It was a five-yard penalty in the books but another 80 yards lost in opportunity cost.

That series began with a loss of three by Rawls because of something the Seahawks never figured out in three years with Jimmy Graham. He *can't* block. When Graham came to Seattle, he was asked about his blocking ability. He said something like, "I'm 6' 7" and 240 pounds, I think I can do it." No, he couldn't. And the crime wasn't his inability to block. It was that they put him in situations where it was vital for him to block. This was the case on that run that went nowhere and a source for the frustration that year when it came to play calling.

The next play, Rees Odhiambo, a rookie third-round draft choice who was filling in for a rookie first-round draft choice in Germain Ifedi, stepped on Wilson's foot on the snap of the ball, causing him to fall backward into the end zone for a safety. Again, luck was running out. They lost 36–20 their second biggest margin since Bobby Wagner and Russell Wilson arrived in 2012, and it was certainly their biggest playoff loss.

The Seahawks were frustrated in the end, and it was playing out on the field with a few scraps as time ran out. After the game Chancellor discussed the state of the team, particularly the defense. "There were lots of distractions, plays we normally make [that] we didn't make," he said.

"I told the guys every game that we argue and fight the other team, we lose. You gotta remain poised. Keep your focus and energy and move on to the next play. We need to look at ourselves in the mirror."

It was as straightforward as I have ever seen a player be. Chancellor was absolutely right—there was way too much energy spent after the whistle blew. Leaders like Chancellor are rare. It's a shame that a leader like that would not be there for them the same time next year.

CHAPTER 13

2017 AND THE LEGION OF BOOM BEGINS TO GO BUST

As the 2017 season began, it seemed all anyone could still talk about was the Seahawks not having beaten the New England Patriots almost two-and-a-half years earlier in the Super Bowl. Perhaps part of the Super Bowl hangover was not just the divvying up of credit, but also about pointing the finger of blame. Russell Wilson did throw the game-losing interception in Super Bowl XLIX. It was amazing that this was still being thought about. It was almost three years later, and some people couldn't let it go.

If it was still about that interception, hadn't the defense given up two fourth-quarter touchdown drives that went for more than 60 yards each in that same game? But proof that the devastating defeat still lingered came that offseason in an article on ESPN.com that stated there were some players who felt that Wilson was treated more favorably by Pete Carroll and that he was coddled by Carroll and the organization.

The article began with an anecdote detailing a day when Richard Sherman picked off Wilson in practice, handed him the ball, and said, "You fucking suck!" Sherman was told not to do that (presumably by Carroll). But the players, who thought like Sherm, felt the coaches were making Wilson one of their own. There were even players who felt that Carroll called a play that would give Wilson a better chance of winning MVP than Marshawn Lynch in Super Bowl XLIX.

Before we enter this bizarre and insane wormhole, let's make this clear: offensive coordinator Darrell Bevell called the play. A quick story about my playing days reinforces why I don't believe any conspiracy theories about that play call. On the sidelines as a coach or a player, you don't have much of a handle on statistics. You can only sort of tell who is or isn't playing well. It's easier these days with the photographs or iPads the players look at between series. But for the most part, there's little time to dwell on plays gone by because of the play clock and the urgency of the game. Mistakes get made, but if you've been part of an NFL game, it's an assault on your senses with the noise, action, and the speed of it all.

After planning the whole week, I thought I had an idea of how things would go, but once the game started, it was an explosion of activity. Usually, it's rarely anything close to what you expected during your preparation. Before the advent of technology, it was even tougher. In a game against Arizona early in my career, the Cardinals were gashing us with a particular running play, and when I went to the sidelines, defensive coordinator Tom Catlin asked me, "Who is blocking you?" I replied, "I have no idea!" As he walked away, a flash of an image entered my mind, and I shouted out, "It was a white guy!" This was telling because the guard on my side was white, and the center was black. You react on instincts, and it all doesn't really make sense until you see the film after the game. In that case I remembered a single image of the guy who blocked me on those plays. It was just a flash of a remembrance of a white face behind a gray facemask.

So, it's very unlikely that Carroll had much of a handle on statistics and who was or wasn't in line to be the Super Bowl MVP. Statistics don't matter to coaches during a game. You get a vague sense of what is working and what isn't, but statistics are for after the game. As a player or coach, you don't always see things clearly from ground level on the sidelines either. As a matter of fact, one of the reasons I respect Carroll so much is the way he handles postgame interviews. The one thing you'll hear him say more than anything else is: "I'll have to look at the film."

The whole thing was ridiculous and fell into a category that I call on my radio show: "Things that just get said." In the absence of any rational thought, fans—and even some of the players—jumped on board with "the franchise didn't want Lynch to be named MVP." It was the easiest and laziest explanation, but mostly it was a harsh criticism of a guy like Carroll, who had given Lynch and a lot of players on that team a chance to shine.

Once doubt crept in, it became commonplace to question every move—playing time, draft choices, and who made the Opening Day roster—as the Seahawks headed into the 2017 season. One such instance was the release of receiver Kasen Williams at the end of camp in 2017 when the Seahawks decided instead to keep Tanner McEvoy. I had discussions with someone close to the team about the move to cut Williams and keep McEvoy. He supported the move and believed that, though Williams was a great leaper and will battle hard for a 50/50 ball, McEvoy was a better special-teams player and was more versatile as a receiver.

To exemplify the kind of challenging mind-set Carroll was dealing with, Sherman took to Twitter to rip the move, stating, "There is no explanation for this!" This whole thing was about the last receiver on the roster—basically the 53rd player on a 53-man roster. It showed just how much doubt was creeping in. After Williams' release the NFL sided with the Seahawks. Williams was picked up by the lowly Cleveland Browns and played intermittently in 2017. I was a huge fan of Williams, having coached against him (with very little success) as a defensive coordinator with Interlake High School and Lake Washington High School. He is a great person and an amazing athlete, but he wasn't on a roster in 2018 after having played with both the Browns and Indianapolis Colts since his release from the Seahawks.

But again, once doubt crept in, some players let their minds wander. The great Cortez Kennedy had a saying: "Players play, coaches coach, and owners own." Translation: stay in your lane.

Furthermore, every team I was ever on, the quarterback was always treated differently. Carroll treating Wilson differently than the rest of the team was nothing new. Your average starting quarterback in the NFL is typically closer to the coaches and the management than he is to the players. It's just how it is. You won't find a quarterback getting in fights with teammates or out with the guys drinking beer and bitching about the coaches. They're different.

Besides that, Wilson *was* performing. Sure, he made mistakes just like any NFL quarterback, but he was setting NFL records in between those mistakes. Heading into the 2019 season, he's had 27 fourth-quarter and overtime come-from-behind wins (tied for the most with Matthew Stafford of the Detroit Lions). Wilson was the first quarterback to have winning seasons in each of his first seven years.

Certainly, he was the beneficiary of excellent defense from guys like Sherman and enjoyed a top five running game because of Lynch.

But it's hard to ignore records like this: Wilson is the second quarterback in NFL history to have 3,000-plus yards passing and 20 or more touchdown passes in each of his first seven seasons. The first to do it? The great Peyton Manning. On top of that, he did it with 619 *fewer* pass attempts. Wilson has averaged 29 pass attempts per game his first seven years in the league, and Manning averaged 34 pass attempts during that same period. Does this sound like a player that the coaches need to yell at?

Every person in America bitches about his or her workplace. There have been disgruntled employees since the beginning of time. I myself bitched nearly every day about having to write this book. (Editor's note: indeed he did.) But I soldiered on because I agreed to do it. The complaining from the Seahawks was different. It wasn't like the normal complaining that you hear from people who work together. It was more like a family splitting up.

It was tough to hear about this stuff because everyone loved Sherman, myself included, for putting the Seahawks on the map and coming up with big play after big play. On the other side was Wilson. How can you not love Wilson? It was like being a child in a divorce and having to choose between Mommy or Daddy. Knowing that was brewing under the surface took the luster away from this entirely lovable team.

* * *

The 2017 draft would end up being one with a cautionary tale involved. The Seahawks took a chance on a player who was a bit of a gamble. A fantastically talented player out of Michigan State who I thought might surprise everyone, Malik McDowell never made it to even one practice. The knock on him was that he would take plays off. In other words, he didn't play hard on every down. But he wasn't even 21 years old yet, so the thought was that he could change. So the Seahawks took a chance by drafting him in the second round, which was their first pick in the draft.

The Seahawks do an amazing job of advising players and taking care of them off the field. Maurice Kelly was a player for the Seahawks in the early 2000s and has served as the vice president of player development for 15 years. One of the things that they do is to bring in the newly drafted college players and their families to educate them on all of the benefits, opportunities, and trappings that go along with being an NFL player. The most solemn piece of advice conveyed to all is that the months between the draft and signing your contract are when you will be most vulnerable as a professional athlete. You don't get the bulk of your money until you pass your physical and sign your contract. So be careful.

Unfortunately, McDowell took a joy ride on the streets of Detroit in an all-terrain vehicle and was involved in a nearly fatal accident that left him unable to play football—possibly permanently. It's a tragedy. It could happen to anyone. I do believe he took an unnecessary risk, but it could happen in a car accident, or you could get hit by a bus. I thought about similar risks that I took in the offseason—not ever thinking it would end my career. I jet skied, surfed, played basketball, and drove too fast in my car. I suppose that could've been me or anyone else. We'll never know what McDowell could've done, but it's a shame, and every time an incident like that occurs, I can't help but think what if Walter Jones or Bobby Wagner was involved in an accident like this?

But if McDowell was the tragedy in the 2017 draft, there were some players whose stories are on their way to having much happier endings. Specifically, two players both from the state of Oklahoma could be the story of this draft for years to come. Chris Carson (Oklahoma State) and David Moore (East Central Oklahoma) were both drafted in the seventh round and both are the type of player that make me call the draft a "crapshoot" every year. The number of players, who were either late-round draft choices or undrafted free agents and have gone on to success, is astonishing to me. But you could probably find more players on the other end of the spectrum—first-round draft choices that were flops.

Moore and, especially Carson, fit the mold of players that make it in the NFL. An old radiomate of mine and legendary Seattle Supersonics broadcaster, Kevin Calabro, used to call guys like that "PHDs" because they were poor, hungry, and driven. I'm not so sure about poor these days, but hungry and driven is what you see when a receiver goes back in the game with a dislocated finger and blood in his glove and catches a game-winning touchdown pass—as Paul Richardson once did.

Carson was also one of four players the Seahawks were able to get from the extra picks acquired by trading down to get McDowell, meaning the legacy of that move may look better down the road than

okie running back Chris Carson rushes for a chunk of his 93 yards during a Week 2 victory against the n Francisco 49ers.

it did when the reports first surfaced of his accident and injury. The draft haul was part of John Schneider and Pete Carroll going full steam ahead to try to win another Super Bowl. They also brought in a number of veterans to try to reload. Blasts from the past included offensive lineman Luke Joeckel and defensive end Dion Jordan. They had been the second and third overall choices in the 2013 draft, and obviously their careers had not gone the way they thought, considering their draft slot. But the Seahawks were hoping maybe each could finally reach their potential in Seattle.

They also signed running back Eddie Lacy from the Green Bay Packers. He had been a Pro Bowler with the Packers and had twice surpassed 1,000 yards and was hopefully the cure for their running game that took a drastic nose dive in 2016. What ended up being the best move was one that wasn't greeted with a lot of fanfare when it was made—signing Tampa Bay Buccaneers safety Bradley McDougald.

Their last move before the season started was to trade Jermaine Kearse and a 2018 draft pick to the New York Jets for defensive lineman Sheldon Richardson. It was clear that the Seahawks felt they were just a few players away from making another run at the Super Bowl. With contracts coming due on players such as Richard Sherman and the overall aging of the roster, the future was now. I am a fan of Kearse, but I understood the move, and though it took a while for Sheldon Richardson to get going, in the end he probably contributed more to the team than Kearse could have.

While the Seahawks were hoping for a return to the Super Bowl in 2017, a lot of things got in the way to turn the season off course. One that may have proved bigger than football—players who felt compelled to use their public platform to bring attention to social injustice.

Throughout the Carroll era, the Seahawks had a number of high-profile players who spoke their minds whenever asked about any number of issues. When it came to some of the major issues facing our country, it only made sense that some of the Seahawks would want to make their voices heard.

The one who spoke the loudest was Michael Bennett, who began sitting for the national anthem as the 2017 season began, and in the beginning, he was one of a few players around the league who was following the lead of former San Francisco quarterback Colin Kaepernick. The protests were viewed differently by seemingly everyone. On one side it was: "How can you disrespect our country and those who have fought and died for your right to protest?" On the other was: "So you're saying you don't want equality in this country and better treatment from the police?" There were also people who didn't want their sports served with a side dish of politics. Even some of the players were divided on the protests. It wasn't about the issue itself as much as it was about how much focus and time were being spent on handling the national anthem.

My idea was for the NFL and the players to agree to stop the protests in return for Social Justice Awareness month—just as they do in October every year for Breast Cancer Awareness month. Owners and fans and players alike could donate to the players' preferred causes. That would not only bring focus and money to the players' favorite causes, but also stop what many felt was a bad look.

But no one was listening to me, so it continued to be a point of contention between the players and the fans. As the season went on, the protests by players became a bigger and bigger issue. It got to the point where reporters were scanning the sidelines from the press box with their binoculars during the anthem to see who was protesting. It peaked in Week 3 when President Trump criticized the players and their protests and it was rumored that the Seahawks, who were one of the more outspoken teams on the subject, had hours of meetings before the Tennessee Titans game to decide what they were going to do about it. Ultimately, the Seahawks and Titans each decided they would stay inside their locker rooms during the anthem and then take the field together as a team. Whether that was a distraction big enough to lose the game for the Seahawks is unknown. The Seahawks were within two points at the half and lost by just six points.

What we knew for sure was that the loss dropped Seattle's record to 1–2—the Seahawks had a sloppy loss to Green Bay to start the year—and nothing about the season seemed to be going according to plan. Although they were 1–2 to start the season, the Seahawks did what they have always done—they went on a run. That involved doing what the Seahawks had done best: getting takeaways on defense. During their four-game streak in the month of October, the Seahawks defense took the ball away 11 times, two of them for touchdowns.

It started against the Indianapolis Colts in a *Sunday Night Football* game they won 46–18. In that game cornerback Justin Coleman picked off a pass for a touchdown. Coleman had been dealt to the Seahawks from the New England Patriots for a seventh-round pick. Coleman turned out to be one of my favorite players that year and still is, though he's now on the Detroit Lions. He is not a big guy, but he covered the pass, played the run, took on blocks, tackled, covered punts, and even scored touchdowns. Coleman is a baller.

Another significant play was a 30-yard touchdown run by running back J.D. McKissic. It would turn out to be the only rushing touchdown the Seahawks would score all season by someone other than quarterback Russell Wilson, an odd statistic that would be talked about all offseason and into the start of 2018.

As good as the win was, it was soured by the injury of Carson. The seventh-round rookie ran well in the preseason, and I felt he would not only make the team, but also be the starter in Week 1. And indeed he was the starter in Week 1, having beaten out heralded free-agent signee Lacy and holdover Thomas Rawls, and was the leading rusher up to the point of his injury. It was a shame because you could see that he was starting to get it. A few times he was one read of a block or one cut right or left away from busting a big one. He was on the verge of breaking out when he went down with a broken leg.

The next week they beat the resurgent Rams in Los Angeles 16–10. The Seahawks defense took the ball away five times, and safety Earl Thomas was part of two of them, including a crucial forced fumble.

Running back Todd Gurley was headed for the pylon and a potential touchdown on the Rams' first possession of the game when Thomas slapped the ball out of his hand, causing Gurley to lose control of the ball and fumble it out of the side of the end zone for a touchback.

It was a play that exemplified the saying: "It's a game of inches." It also exemplified how tenacious and skilled Thomas is. He could've swiped at the ball or just tried to tackle Gurley. Watching it on instant replay, it appeared that Thomas was aiming for that exact point in space and took the most direct line to that intersection while slapping the ball out in a precise manner that only All-Pro players can execute.

One of the pleasant surprises that season was Paul Richardson, a receiver out of Colorado who was taken in the second round of the 2014 draft. By mid-season he had five touchdown catches, and none was more impressive than the one he caught against the San Francisco 49ers in Week 2. In the first quarter, he had broken his finger so badly that the bone stuck through his skin. When he took his glove off to show the doctor, the glove was full of blood. As told to us on *Danny, Dave and Moore* on 710 ESPN Seattle, the doctor wanted him to go into the locker room to examine the finger and sew it up. He told the doctor, "I'm not going in unless you promise me that I can come back in the game." Luckily, the doctor kept his word, and Richardson caught the game-winner with his freshly sewn-up hand. Just as I said about Coleman, Richardson is a football player. He's in it for everything, or as Schneider likes to say, "He's all ball."

For Richardson's sake, I was happy to see that in the next free-agency period he was too expensive for the Seahawks and signed a lucrative contract with the Washington Redskins. I didn't want to see him go, but the Seahawks wanted to run the ball more than pass it, and the Redskins rightfully saw something special in Richardson.

The Seahawks saw something special in left tackle Duane Brown, who was not happy in Houston, and the Texans were looking for a trade partner. The fourth game in that winning streak brought him to town, and the Seahawks got a good look at him. It was impressive. He had some traits that reminded you of the GOAT—Walter Jones. He was always under control, had great feet under his massive body, was strong, and never looked desperate or out of control. Two days later the Seahawks traded Jeremy Lane and their 2018 and 2019 second-round draft choices to the Texans for Brown. It was a great trade, and before the 2018 season, the Seahawks extended Brown's contract for three more years, paying him just less than $12 million per year.

The quarterback he was protecting that day, the Texans' Deshaun Watson, had the same winning characteristics as Brown and had won a national championship for Clemson by making a clutch play in the end vs. Alabama. Unfortunately, that was the version of Watson the Seahawks would face. He threw more than 400 yards, but not before the Legion of Boom picked him off three times. (Thomas had one interception, and Sherman had two.) The Seahawks pulled off a 41–38 win.

* * *

Glendale, Arizona, was the scene of the Seahawks' greatest heartbreak in 2015, and it proved to be similar in Week 10 of the 2017 season. By halftime the Seahawks defense had given up just 90 yards and seven points against the Arizona Cardinals, and Kam Chancellor had forced a fumble and tackled running back Adrian Peterson in Arizona's end zone for a safety.

The hard-running Peterson was in Arizona that year, and Chancellor, who was up on the line of scrimmage like a linebacker, shuffled down the line with perfect technique that most linebackers can't execute and stoned Peterson in the backfield. The forced fumble was similar. He was again lined up on the line of scrimmage and fought off a block by a tight end and popped the ball out of the running back's hands. He would've had a fumble recovery later in the half, but because of the NFL's ridiculous catch rule, the pass was ruled incomplete, even though the ball carrier had taken at least three steps.

Chancellor finished the game with 10 tackles, a forced fumble, and the safety. The last of those tackles, though, proved to be the last of his career—a seemingly innocuous hit on Arizona running back Andre Ellington with just more than two minutes left. No one even knew Chancellor was hurt; he stayed in for one more play before departing, and most just thought the Seahawks were getting him out of the game to get out of harm's way.

Chancellor felt something wasn't right in his neck, an injury that was later diagnosed as spinal stenosis. Carroll mentioned the injury in passing after the game, and few really thought much of it. That's because all the focus was on Richard Sherman, who was done for the year when he crumpled to the ground in the third quarter with a torn Achilles. His reaction—and that of everyone on the sidelines—made it clear this was a serious injury.

Because the game was played on a Thursday night just four days after their loss to the Washington Redskins, it brought to the surface a lot of complaints from the players about playing a game on short rest. I don't disagree with them. There's lots of money on the line so I understand why the NFL schedules Thursday night games, but there was plenty in this game, especially Sherman's worn-down Achilles, that demonstrated what the players were complaining about.

Without Sherman and Chancellor, the Legion of Boom looked drastically different. Only defensive backs Earl Thomas and Jeremy Lane remained from the players who had been with the team in the Super Bowl era. Lane took over for Sherman, and Bradley McDougald took over Chancellor's spot at strong safety. McDougald had taken a chance signing with the Seahawks. He had a starting job with the Tampa Bay Buccaneers and was a good pro on the verge of a breakout season. He knew that signing with Seattle would cut into his playing time, but both sides were confident he would get a chance to start. When the Seahawks signed him, there wasn't much said about him.

I got a phone call from general manager John Schneider a week or so after he signed McDougald, and he asked me why we weren't talking about McDougald more on the radio. He told me, "This signing is a big deal, and Bradley is a big-time player." It turned out he was right. McDougald stepped right in without much drop off at both strong and free safety. He helped bolster a defensive backfield that was suddenly very depleted.

While he shored up that position, the kicker was a very different situation. The kicker is one of three positions you don't want to have to talk or worry about. Another one is cornerback. Outside of quarterback, playing corner in the NFL is the most difficult position in professional football. You play out on an island—often with no help and against wide receivers, some of whom are the most freakishly talented athletes on the planet. Guys like Larry Fitzgerald, Anquan Boldin, and Julio Jones are usually 6'4," run 4.4 40s, and can jump out of the stadium. I don't believe shut-down corners exist. If you play corner in the league, you will get beat. Even good ones like Sherman don't shut everyone down. But you typically don't have to worry about them either. For example, in 2016 versus the New York Jets, Sherman had a duel with 6'5" Brandon Marshall, one of those freakish receivers. At halftime Marshall had three catches for 72 yards and a touchdown all against Sherman. In the second half, Marshall had one catch, and Sherman picked off two passes that were both meant for Marshall.

The blind-side offensive tackle (or left tackle for the Seahawks) is another position you worry about because you don't want your quarterback to get hit in the back of the head, and he typically blocks an edge rusher, the second most freaky athlete in the league. Guys like Cliff Avril, Von Miller, and Khalil Mack are 250-plus pounds, can run like the wind, and turn a tight corner at full speed. For most of recent Seahawks history, Seattle has gone from Hall of Famer Walter Jones, to first-rounder and Pro Bowler Russell Okung, to Pro Bowler Duane Brown. There's not much to worry about there.

Then…there's the kicker. You should know that I don't consider kickers to be football players. They're kickers. This is why I gave a pass to Sebastian Janikowski for not tackling a kick returner in a game in

2018 against the San Francisco 49ers. Yes, it appeared that he was jogging off the field to get a Gatorade instead of breaking down and at least re-routing the return man, but he's a kicker, and anything else would've been asking him to do something that the young athletic defensive backs and linebackers should've been doing. The kickers kick. They don't tackle or run or jump or throw. The end.

Like the Seahawks' good fortune with left tackles, they also had been blessed with a good kicker during their championship era. Stephen Hauschka had performed well in key situations in that era. But in 2016 he had missed a chip shot in Arizona that resulted in a 6–6 tie. It was in a stadium where he had missed often. After that miss he reportedly complained to his holder, punter Jon Ryan, that he didn't like the grass down there. Ryan reportedly responded, "Dude, you didn't even hit the fucking net." It wasn't the grass, even though the Seahawks seem to be cursed in University of Arizona stadium.

My radio co-host, Danny O'Neil, compares kickers to spoiled milk. If you pull milk out of the refrigerator and it stinks, it's not going to get any fresher. By the 2017 offseason, the Seahawks took a whiff of Hauschka and moved on. For whatever reason they then turned to free agent Blair Walsh, which was an odd choice because he was the kicker who had also missed a chip shot in the 2016 playoffs that sent the Seahawks to the second round of the playoffs.

Walsh, however, had also set an NFL record with 12 straight makes of 50 yards or longer earlier in his career. And the Seahawks were hoping that was the version of Walsh they would get. They were hoping for the version who had once made the Pro Bowl and not the one who missed the 27-yarder in the playoffs. Sadly, they got the latter.

In 2017 Walsh missed five kicks in three games that they would've won or tied—had the milk not been spoiled. He missed three in a 17–14 loss to the Redskins. He missed another one—though it was from more than 50 yards—in a game they lost to the Atlanta Falcons 34–31 and one more at the end of a 26–24 loss in the last game of the season against the

Cardinals. Carroll had an I-can't-believe-that-really-happened look after Walsh missed against the Cardinals. No one else could believe it either.

More than kicking woes, injuries and the lack of a consistent running game—something the Seahawks were used to going their way—started to catch up to them down the stretch in 2017, and it became evident there might be some major changes coming. The injury list had key players on it. Along with Sherman and Chancellor, Cliff Avril was on that list with a career-ending spinal injury that occurred in Week 4. Chris Carson went down with a broken leg that same week. George Fant, who had made an amazing transition from college basketball player to offensive tackle, also went down with a knee injury and was gone for the year. At key points players like K.J. Wright and Bobby Wagner missed games as well, and that proved to be too much for the Seahawks to overcome.

The running game—such a key to everything from 2012 to 2015—didn't help either. Eight times that year, the Seahawks did not rush for more than 100 yards and finished as the 23rd best running game, averaging just more than 100 yards per game. Of the 38 touchdowns the team scored in 2017, Wilson was part of 37 of them running and throwing. It was an amazing feat for him, but a stat that said way too much about the Seattle offense that season.

It all caught up to them in a late-season game that looked to everyone watching as a changing of the guard in the NFC West. When the injury report came out before a game against a resurgent Los Angeles Rams team that was on its way to winning the division, Wright was out because of a concussion he had suffered the week before in a 24–30 loss at the Jacksonville Jaguars, and Wagner was listed as questionable but played anyway. But on a 57-yard run by Rams running back Todd Gurley, it was obvious that Wagner was not 100 percent. Neither were the Seahawks, who were routed 42–7 for the worst loss of the Carroll era.

In my mind, football is a game that is not about percentage of health. You hear analysts and writers say that someone is at 70 percent.

To me it's like a rocket launch from Cape Canaveral. You're either a "Go" or a "No Go." You can't play at 70 percent, and based on what I saw from Wagner on that play, he was 70 percent. But this was not on Wagner. Every player, who is worth his salt, is going to try to play. I remember trying to fool Chuck Knox before a game in 1990 and convince him that I was healthy enough to go. He didn't fall for it, and it was definitely better for the team. So I was surprised that the Seahawks didn't hold Wagner out of that game. Thomas seemed to put the blame on Wagner, noting after the game that some guys tried to play who maybe shouldn't have. "The backups would have done just as good," he said. It was a valiant effort by Wagner, and he did what any player would do in that situation. He tried to play—health be damned.

While fighting to stay in the playoff hunt, the Seahawks beat the Philadelphia Eagles handily with a 24–10 win in a Week 13 in a *Sunday Night Football* game in Seattle. The Eagles were arguably the best team in the NFL, which they would prove a few weeks later by winning the Super Bowl. That made it all the more surprising when the Seahawks got blown out by the Rams. It was equally surprising that the Seahawks won the next week on the road against the Dallas Cowboys. The Seahawks won based partly on a Justin Coleman pick-6 when he jumped a Dak Prescott throw and then jumped into the Salvation Army kettle in the end zone. Although he was fined for the celebration, it was one of the better moments that year.

It was a win that no one expected after what had happened against the Rams, but the surprise factor paled in comparison to what happened after the game. Thomas, who is from Texas and was unhappy that the Seahawks had not talked to him about extending his contract, followed Cowboys head coach Jason Garrett into the Dallas locker room and shouted, "If you have a chance to get me, come get me."

I felt like the pulse in Seattle was that people loved Thomas so much that they were willing to forgive him. Thomas can be kind of spacey, and when he did things like that, fans and teammates alike would write it off as: "Well, that's just Earl being Earl."

In 2018 I traveled with the team to Carolina, where Seahawks great—and my former teammate and the Seahawks' all-time leading tackler, Eugene Robinson—is the color commentator on the Panthers' broadcasts. In a conversation before the game he asked me, "Hey, did Earl really follow Garrett into the locker room and ask them to come get him after a game?" He was amazed by the lack of allegiance, and that kind of brought me around to how bad it was. I spoke of Marshawn Lynch's insubordination by not getting on the bus to a road playoff game without telling the coaches. My conversation with Robinson made me realize Thomas' transgression might have been worse.

The season ended with a thud when the Seahawks lost their last game, and it was a home game, but it wasn't just because of a missed Walsh field goal. This team had lost the spirit that Chancellor, Sherman, and Avril brought to the table. Immediatly following their shutout win against the New York Giants the week before, Cardinals head coach Bruce Arians was talking shit to the team that was used to having an upper hand in that category. "We know that's our home field," Arians told his players in the locker room, according to azcentral.com. "We're going up there and kick their asses."

After word of this was leaked out, Arians doubled down on it. "Things that you say to your team in your locker room are supposed to be in your locker room," Arians told reporters. "But it got out. I said it, so…we have won three times in a row up there."

This would've got under the skin of players like Sherman and inspired them, but the Seahawks had lost their way, and it was obvious that a rebuilding of the team was necessary in the offseason. For the first time in their championship era, the 9–7 Seahawks did not get double digit wins nor make the playoffs.

CHAPTER 14

STARTING OVER IN 2018

If there was a theme going into the 2018 offseason from Pete Carroll and John Schneider, it was: "Screw it. We'll do it all over again with young guys." It's a wise strategy with the rookie salaries being what they are these days in the NFL compared to what the veterans make. Russell Wilson played for about $700,000 a season during his first three years, which gave the Seahawks a huge and rare advantage in how it could put together the rest of its team in the challenging salary cap era. Rebuilding with young guys, though, is easier said than done.

Some of the changes, however, were forced on the Seahawks, such as the career-ending injuries to Cliff Avril and Kam Chancellor. It was painful when the Seahawks released Avril and put Chancellor on the physically-unable-to-perform list. Both players had been a huge part of what the Seahawks had accomplished defensively and both were great leaders who would be sorely missed. But it was a pretty easy decision for both of them, considering they each were facing spinal cord issues. Avril has a nice little family started, and as most NFL players will tell you, they want to be able to play with their kids in the backyard someday.

The Seahawks also traded Michael Bennett to the Philadelphia Eagles and released Richard Sherman. Both were not happy here anymore and took their potshots at Carroll on their way out. Sherman said that Carroll's message was stale, and Bennett claimed to have read books during Carroll's team meetings, presumably because they were so boring. Part of the problem in Seattle, according to Sherman, was that Carroll was saying the same things over and over again. You think I didn't listen to the same stuff from Chuck Knox year after year? That's what coaches do—especially if it's working. Whatever boring things Carroll was saying, it would've been criminal for him to *not* say them over and over again. *A historically good defense, five years of double-digit wins, trips to the playoffs for five years in a row, two Super Bowl appearances, and one Super Bowl title?* I wish my NFL coaches had been that boring!

After being released and then signing with Seattle's archrival San Francisco 49ers, which even he admitted was done in part so he could face the Seahawks twice a year, Sherman said he also thought the franchise had "lost its way." You know Carroll and Schneider wanted to prove otherwise.

Another offseason theme for Schneider and Carroll was that they were not going to dive into free agency and throw millions of dollars around, something they have rarely done anyway, preferring to build their teams from the ground up. Even the signings of Bennett and Avril in 2013 were second-tier signings. Other than the two big splashy deals for Jimmy Graham and Percy Harvin, the Seahawks have mostly used free agency to fill in the bottom end of their depth chart. Signings over the years for guys like Ahtyba Rubin, Mike Davis, and Barkevious Mingo for modest numbers in the $2 to $4 million range was their gameplan.

Mingo was an interesting player Seattle added in 2018. He had been the sixth pick of the draft in 2013 out of LSU. The edge rusher had struggled in the first five years of his career, compiling just nine sacks, so the Seahawks signed him to a two-year, reasonably priced contract.

Their thinking was that players like him could revitalize their careers and fit a specific need for the team all for a reasonable price. For Mingo it meant standing up, not putting his hand in the dirt, and playing linebacker, which he did well in the '18 season. He was also arguably their best player on special teams.

The 2018 season was also notable for Carroll making the first major changes to his assistant coaching staff in his time in Seattle. Defensive coordinator Gus Bradley had moved on to get a head coaching job with the Jacksonville Jaguars in 2012. Bradley's replacement, Dan Quinn, took the Atlanta Falcons' head coaching job in 2015. But there hadn't been wholesale changes like this. Gone were offensive line coach Tom Cable, offensive coordinator Darrell Bevell, and defensive coordinator Kris Richard. It's obvious Carroll takes pride in developing coaches and helping them get to the next level. I've never seen a head coach more interested in helping his assistants leave on a good note, so I'm sure it was tough for him having to let four coaches go.

But something needed to be done, and the most significant move was bringing Ken Norton back as the defensive coordinator. Norton has been with Carroll since 2004 at USC and then left in '15 to be the defensive coordinator for the Oakland Raiders. If you ask Norton about Carroll, he typically says, "Pete is my guy." There's a strong connection there that flows both ways, and when the Seahawks had a chance to go back to the future, they jumped on it.

I saw the offensive coaching changes this way—they basically fired the running game. Bevell and Cable (as well as running back coach Sherman Smith, who was let go the year before) all had their fingerprints on the recent woes in the running game that had plummeted to the bottom third of the league in 2016–17. This was curious because their fingerprints were also all over the 2012–15 seasons that had top four running games every year. The 2014 team even led the NFL in not only rushing yards and touchdowns, but also rushing yards per attempt while ranking second in attempts. In other words, even though teams knew the running game was coming, they still couldn't stop it.

But it was sort of like the running game worked great until it just stopped—seemingly overnight. No doubt that Marshawn Lynch's absence certainly played a role—as did the demolition of the offensive line that won the Super Bowl. By 2016 every single one of those guys was gone. But Carroll also felt that coaching changes needed to be made after the 2017 season.

So they promoted assistant running back coach Chad Morton to running backs coach, brought offensive line coach Mike Solari back to Seattle for his second stint after coaching in Seattle from 2008 to 2009, and hired offensive coordinator Brian Schottenheimer. It worked. Schottenheimer was given some grief by the media early on when he said you need to have "the ability to run the football when people know you are going to run."

I may have been one of the few people in the media who understood exactly what Schottenheimer meant. I played in the late 1980s and early '90s against Brian's dad, Marty Schottenheimer, who was then the head coach of the Kansas City Chiefs. They had a huge offensive line with guys like John Alt, who was 6'8", 300 pounds, and after you took him on, they ran at you with Christian Okoye. The "Nigerian Nightmare" was 6'1" and 250 pounds. You just hoped to hold on and limit them to under five yards per carry. At its most basic level, the running game is about imposing your will on the other team. And I can tell you from personal experience: when a team throws the ball down the field and scores, it's not nearly as demoralizing as a 15-play scoring drive where they run it down your throat and take nine minutes off the clock.

It became clear what Schottenheimer meant when they signed a couple of road graders in offensive guards D.J. Fluker and J.R. Sweezy, who would end up leading a back like 5'11", 222-pound Chris Carson right down opponents' throats in 2018. Seattle again led the NFL in rushing—just the way Carroll likes it.

*   *   *

The 2018 draft was vintage John Schneider. Of course, the jury is still out on just how it will turn out. But it has the look of shaping into a 2012-like draft, meaning it was loaded with selections that most people panned. Like 2012 it was another "Island of Misfit Toys" draft. In the 2012 NFL Draft, no one thought Bruce Irvin was a first-rounder, and everyone thought Russell Wilson was too short. Bobby Wagner was from a small football program, and J.R. Sweezy was a defensive tackle drafted to play offensive guard.

Six years later this draft included a running back that no one had ranked as a first rounder (Rashaad Penny) and also featured a move up to draft a punter (Michael Dickson). There was also a fourth-round tight end (Will Dissily) out of the great state of Montana who was originally a defensive lineman at University of Washington. There was a one-handed linebacker (Shaquem Griffin), who was the twin brother of a Shaquill Griffin, and a tall, lanky safety who they drafted to play cornerback (Tre Flowers).

My favorite moment was when the Seahawks selected Shaquem in the fifth round. Shaquem was an incredibly productive player at University of Central Florida and had been American Athletic Conference Defensive Player of the Year in 2016 while playing alongside Shaquill. That year Shaquem had 92 tackles, two forced fumbles, two fumble recoveries, 11.5 sacks, and an interception. Still, there were lots of questions about whether he could play in the NFL.

That's because he was born with Amniotic Band Syndrome. A strand in the amniotic sac was wrapped around his left wrist, and because of that, the fingers on his left hand would not develop properly and caused him a severe amount of pain. By the time he was four years old, his left hand was in so much pain that his mother found him in the kitchen, attempting to use a butcher's knife to amputate his own hand so that he could get rid of the pain once and for all. His parents scheduled an amputation the next day.

The Griffin brothers played football together their whole lives, and when it was time to be recruited out of high school, Shaquill was the more sought-after player. But Shaquill made it known they were a package deal. Even though Shaquill's dream school was the University of Miami, he turned down an offer there so he could play with his brother at UCF. The Seahawks made Shaquill their third-round pick in the 2017 draft while Shaquem stayed at UCF and helped them go undefeated as part of a legendary winning streak that would eventually stretch to 25 games.

When invites were initially sent out for the NFL Combine, the event held every year in Indianapolis where pro teams scout the top college talent, Shaquem's name was not on the list.

Eventually, he was invited and ran the fastest 40-yard dash time for a linebacker (4.38) since 2003. At the end of the 2017 season, the Seahawks played the Jaguars in Jacksonville, and Shaquem was down on the field before the game to see his brother. I looked at Shaquem in awe and asked Schneider if he thought Shaquem could play in the NFL. His response at that time was that he didn't know. That's not something you hear from Schneider very often. But it was understandable. There was no precedent for this. Predictions on draft day ranged from as high as the third round to undrafted.

The day of the draft, I was with a few of my Seahawks colleagues hosting a draft party. Former Seahawks offensive tackle and good friend Ray Roberts and I were fascinated by Shaquem. We went back and forth. "How could you not draft such a productive player?" "How could you draft a player without a left hand?" When the Seahawks picked Shaquem, Roberts and I looked at each other wide-eyed and simultaneously said, "They did it!" It was truly a special moment, and I still get goose bumps when I think about it.

I remember what it meant for me to play with my older brother, Mike, in high school and in college. For these brothers who had done everything together their whole lives, it was special.

At the conclusion of training camp, newly hired defensive coordinator Ken Norton had a very high opinion of this rookie class. He described them this way: "They show up early, they stay late, they work hard, they ask questions, and they don't complain."

That's high praise when coming from a guy like Norton. Every once in a while, I ask players, especially linebackers, "Do you know how good Ken Norton was?" It's impressive to me that Norton, who could sit around and rest on his laurels based on his career, is totally committed to making today's players better. There aren't a lot of Hall of Fame-caliber coaches in the NFL. The coaches that do make it in the NFL tend to be backup quarterbacks like Sean Payton, Jason Garrett, Doug Pederson, and Gary Kubiak. Norton had a very productive, 13-year career, winning three Super Bowls (and in consecutive years with two different teams) and was a three-time Pro Bowler and also a 1995 All-Pro.

With Michael Bennett and Richard Sherman gone, it was a much happier training camp. The feeling of hope for the future was back just like the days of 2012 when this team was on the brink of the championship era of Seahawks football. But there was one holdover from that era who was making things not so joyful—Earl Thomas. The stellar safety was holding out because he wanted one of two things to happen—an extension on his four-year, $10 million contract, which was up following the 2018 season, or a trade.

Right before the regular season was about to begin, the Dallas Cowboys, the team that Thomas had begged to "come get him" at the end of the 2017 season, offered a second-round draft choice for him. The Seahawks turned it down, and Thomas reported the week before the regular season but not before he sent a warning to the Seahawks and anyone else who would listen. Thomas posted the following on Instagram: "I worked my whole life for this…I've never let me teammates, city, or fans down as long as I've lived and don't plan on starting this weekend. With that being said, the disrespect has been well noted and will not be forgotten. Father Time may have an undefeated record, but best believe I plan on taking him into triple overtime when it comes to my career."

Often in these situations, fans will side with the team, and the players will stand by their teammates. Everyone in that locker room welcomed Thomas back with open arms. And in Week 1 at Denver, Thomas delivered against the Broncos. The Seahawks lost to the Broncos 27–24, but Thomas did his part with five tackles, a broken-up pass, and an interception that gave the Seahawks an early 7–0 lead. After the game while he was being interviewed on television, you could hear his teammates shouting out, "Pay that man!"

Two games later he had the kind of outing that made you think maybe the Seahawks would go ahead and pay him. Maybe he was extra fired up because it was Dallas. Whatever the case may be, Thomas registered seven tackles and two interceptions. But any thought that the Seahawks would pay him quickly dissipated when Thomas announced after the win against the Cowboys: "Yeah, I need to make sure my body is 100 [percent]. I'm invested in myself. Now, if they was invested in me, I'd be out there practicing, but if I feel like anything—and I don't give a damn if it's small, I got a headache—I'm not practicing. But I don't want that to be taken the wrong way."

I remember thinking, *There's no other way to take that, Earl!* That strategy was bound to end badly. When players behave that way, I like to think about how my old head coach Chuck Knox would've handled it. I'm thinking Knox would have fired him on the spot, and if the team was on the road, he would have kicked him off the team plane—perhaps in midair. Pete Carroll, on the other hand, was willing to put up with antics like that. Though he was seen as a coach who let players get away with murder, it worked out over the years with players like Thomas, Sherman, Bennett, and Marshawn Lynch. I think those players have Carroll to thank for that. For example, not many coaches would've traded for Lynch in 2010. Lynch had a three-game suspension because of an arrest for misdemeanor gun charges and two other charges for theft and hit-and-run. An even smaller number of coaches would put up with Sherman openly criticizing coaching decisions through the media.

Carroll has thick skin for sure, but more than anything, it's that he loves and respects the players. Carroll coached with Paul Wiggin for the Minnesota Vikings in the 1980s. Each was an assistant at the time, and Wiggin became one of Carroll's favorite people. I also knew "Wigs," as Carroll refers to him, as he had recruited and coached both me and my brother, Mike. And I saw a lot of the same qualities in Wiggin that I see in Carroll. Like Carroll, he was all about the players, and something he said once reflected how he felt about his guys. A linebacker, who was supposed to get treatment from one of the athletic trainers, was turned down because the time wasn't convenient for the trainer. After the player reported this, Coach Wiggin said, "It seems to me that athletic trainers aren't much of a show without the athletes."

What seemed like a simple statement spoke volumes about how he felt about his players. Carroll has this same view. The players are the show. That comes through in the way he handles his players, and they respect him for that, and it's a big reason why Carroll gets so much out of his team. That's not a universal feeling in the NFL. You'll hear some general managers, scouts, or coaches tear players down. If you're not careful, adversarial relationships are developed. Vilifying the players is bad for business. I think it takes a lot of discipline to keep it positive like Carroll and Schneider do. Whether it's contract disputes, holdouts, or playing time decisions, Carroll and Schneider's love and respect for the players shine through.

And ultimately—and unfortunately, given all that he had meant to the team and the way the city felt about him for so long—it did end badly for Thomas. The next week in Arizona, where bad things tend to happen for the Seahawks, he broke his leg defending a deep pass from the Cardinals near the end zone. A lot of Seahawks fans, myself included, would like to see that friggin' building imploded. It's a House of Horrors. There was the bizarre 6–6 tie in 2016, the most heartbreaking Super Bowl loss in history in Super Bowl XLIX, and the three, members of the Legion of Boom ending their Seahawks careers due to injuries in that building.

But Carroll had done it again. Whereas a lot of coaches would not have put up with Thomas' behavior, Carroll got three interceptions in four games out of Thomas before he went on injured reserve. Thomas' last move as a Seahawks player was to extend his middle finger toward the Seattle sidelines. Later he would confirm that the gesture was indeed for Carroll.

Luckily, Carrol has thick skin because you will never hear anything but praise from Carroll when he talks about his former star safety.

* * *

For all the firing and hiring around the running game, there was little to show for their efforts early on. Part of the problem was that offensive coordinator Brian Schottenheimer was calling passes in running situations. And this was from the guy who essentially said: "You have to be able to run the ball when they know it's coming." The Seahawks ran for just 64 yards against the Denver Broncos and just 74 yards the next week on *Monday Night Football* against the Bears in Chicago.

They lost both games and passed a lot in part because they also fell behind early in each game. When they got back to Seattle, Pete Carroll and Schottenheimer had what each later called a meeting of the minds. Specifically, they decided they were going to make good on what Schottenheimer said shortly after being hired about re-emphasizing the run. And by the end of the year, the running game would be the most improved piece of the Seahawks' game. Seattle ended up leading the NFL in rushing yards per game.

When it comes to the running game, my belief is that the running back is much more responsible than the offensive line, an opinion I know not everyone agrees with. But when it's time to point the finger of blame or divvy up the credit, I believe that 75 percent of it is on the running back. You can blast holes in a defense that you can drive a bus through, but it doesn't do any good unless a back can read the blocks. Once the offensive line and backs got line coach Mike Solari's philosophy, they would run their way to a No. 1 running game. But Carroll's philosophy is more than just run the ball—he wants a punishing running game. And Chris Carson began to fit that bill perfectly in 2018.

Carson ran through, around, over, and under players. He looks like a professional weightlifter and is one of those rare players whom teammates talk about with awe. He surpassed 100 yards six times and seemed like he was responsible for half of the team's highlights in 2018. Twice he hurdled over players successfully. The most spectacular occurred in Carolina in Week 12 against the Panthers. That was a game in which the Panthers defense sold out to stop the run, holding the Seahawks juggernaut of a running game to just 75 yards. The one run that did break free for 16 yards caused everyone in the stadium to say "Oooooh!"

Carson broke through the line and got to the second level, where safety Eric Reid was waiting for him. I think he figured that Reid was going to go low, so Carson's instinct was to hurdle Reid. The safety aimed for his midsection, and when Carson got airborne, his shin caught

Reid's shoulder pad, causing the running back to do a flip with a half twist. I remember being concerned for Carson's health. Guys that big are not meant to be 11 feet in the air! But he landed in superhero fashion with one knee and one hand on the ground and continued to try to gain yardage.

Carson ended the year with 1,151 yards and nine touchdowns despite missing two games. He is easy to root for, and it's not just because his runs are reminiscent of Marshawn Lynch. He's a humble, soft-spoken guy with a lot of the grit Carroll loves. His career had been derailed in high school. He had an offer for a full scholarship to Georgia, "Running Back U," but he blew out his knee his senior year and had to go the junior college route for two years before Oklahoma State offered him a scholarship.

The Seahawks then got him with a seventh-round pick (249th overall) in the 2017 draft. Carroll said on draft day that Carson was a personal favorite of his. The head coach had specifically pointed him out going into the draft, hoping the Seahawks could get him. The 2018 season proved why Carroll had been so excited about him.

The Seahawks' start to the season was less promising. Since 2007 teams that start 0–2 have about an 11 percent chance of making the playoffs. After the loss in Chicago, the Seahawks needed to go 10–4 in order to get to the postseason. And against the odds—and the expectations of not only most around the NFL, but what also felt like most Seahawks fans—that's what they did.

Seattle began to run off wins the rest of the 2018 season. Even when the Seahawks lost, it was a tight affair. Of their six losses in '18, only two were to non-playoff teams—the Broncos in Week 1 and the San Francisco 49ers in Week 15, and each was on the road, and the latter was in a downpour with pretty horrid field conditions. If it's at all possible to have good losses, the Seahawks hung with the 2018 NFC champion Los Angeles Rams in both games. They put up 62 points against the Rams and lost both games by a combined six points and had a chance at the end to win both of them.

As happens in an NFL season, in which a team plays a lot of tight games, there were some games they probably shouldn't have won as well. In Week 12 the Seahawks were 5–5, knowing that they could only lose one more game in order to make the playoffs, and they still had the Minnesota Vikings and Kansas City Chiefs left on the schedule. In Week 12 the Panthers were riding a 10-game home winning streak that went back to the middle of the 2017 season. The Panthers defense shut down Seattle's running game, making it as ineffective as it had been since the first two weeks of the season. So Russell Wilson took over. He completed 71 percent of his passes and threw for 339 yards and two touchdowns in leading the Seahawks to a somewhat improbable win. His most clutch throw was on a go route to receiver David Moore on fourth and 3. The pass flew about 45 yards in the air and could not have been in a better spot. It was one of those plays that had made me trust in Wilson, one of those plays that I used to think, *No...not that! What are you doing?* And then, *Oh yeah...great decision!* It happened so many times that I learned to trust in Wilson.

Trust in Wilson. Help Wilson. Leave Wilson alone. These are a few of the mantras on my radio show that I have implored fans to echo. For whatever reason, Wilson has been doubted, nitpicked, and complained about more than he should be—both nationally and even here in Seattle. I honestly don't understand it. No player is perfect, but Wilson has come close.

He started his career with seven straight winning seasons and is the only player in NFL history to have done so. He's orchestrated 27 fourth-quarter and overtime wins, which is tied with Matthew Stafford for the best in the NFL since he entered the league in 2012. He's never missed even one practice or, even more importantly, a game. (He's missed one play due to injury in his career.) He's made epic throws: the one to Moore and the overtime touchdown pass to Jermaine Kearse in the 2014 NFC Championship Game. He had a 73 percent completion rate and 31 touchdowns from the pocket in 2015.

But he also needs help. In 2016 the Seahawks were the 25th-ranked running game and had more than 100 runs of one yard or fewer. In

The Seahawks lost many of their defensive stars prior to the 2018 season, but they could still rely on linebacker Bobby Wagner, one of the NFL's best defensive players.

2017 the Seahawks were the 23rd-ranked running game, and Wilson scored every touchdown other than one. The Seahawks went 9–7 and missed the playoffs. In both of those years, his pass attempts per game went up, and his quarterback rating went down.

When he does get help, he's great. In 2018 the Seahawks running game was the best in the NFL at 160 yards per game. Wilson was dead last in pass attempts per game (27) and No. 3 in touchdowns (35), quarterback rating (111), and fewest interceptions thrown (7).

Whether it's something he posts online, the products he endorses, or what he wears, Wilson also seem to receive a lot of unnecessary criticism off the field. He and his wife, Ciara, will post things on Facebook, professing their love for each other. It may not be my style, but so what? He doesn't get waylaid by off-the-field problems like many athletes. Maybe he doesn't interact with his teammates like everyone would like (or at least, that's how it was portrayed in *Sports Illustrated*). But as far as I can tell, he tries, and I've never heard him utter a bad word about a teammate, react negatively when someone drops one of his passes, or yell at an offensive lineman for missing a block. I think Wilson is his own person. Sometimes he's sappy, sometimes he's corny, and sometimes he's robotic. But he's been consistently good to the media, a good teammate, and a good man off the field. So leave him alone.

Wilson and the Seahawks won some big games down the stretch, including a *Sunday Night Football* win against the 11–3 Chiefs. Wilson outdueled quarterback phenom Patrick Mahomes, posting a 127 quarterback rating to Mahomes' 103. Seattle finished the regular season 10–6 and was headed to Dallas to play the Cowboys in the wild-card round in a rematch of the team they had beaten 24–13 in Week 3. That win jump-started the 10–4 stretch that got the Seahawks back into the playoffs.

Seattle was as close to full strength as you could be. Both linebacker K.J. Wright and guard J.R. Sweezy were back in the lineup. Wright probably played his most complete game, tallying eight tackles—one for a loss and a spectacular interception in the end zone. But Sweezy and the running game could not run the ball on the Cowboys defense, rushing for just 73 yards—less than half of their season average.

There was a lot of criticism of Schottenheimer for not going away from the run more quickly when the Seattle offense failed to move it consistently in the first half. I felt, though, like Schotty couldn't win. He'd been criticized for not committing to the run in Weeks 1 and 2 when Seattle lost on the road at Denver and Chicago and then for running too much in the playoffs. When you have the No. 1 running game in the NFL, you don't just desert the run after two quarters of play. And throughout the year, Carroll said one of his big regrets was straying from the run in those first two games when Seattle fell behind.

The Seahawks were going to dance with what "brung them" to the playoffs and later they would point out that they had the lead in the fourth quarter—14–10. It was developing in their eyes as the kind of game they had been winning all season—if not for much of Carroll's time with the Seahawks—when they seemed to get stronger as the game wore on. Only this time the defense couldn't hold on, as a long Dallas drive gave the lead right back to the Cowboys. Many fans seemed to overlook later that the Seahawks then did nothing but pass the ball the rest of the way. They threw the ball on all but one play after falling behind 17–14. But it just wasn't that simple. They had two straight three-and-outs with a couple of penalties also getting in the way, and the Cowboys were able to hang on for the win.

Everyone questions things after a loss, and Carroll said later that they would have done some things differently if he could do it over. One thing he particularly regretted was that the offensive line wasn't healthy—guards Sweezy and D.J. Fluker each played with injuries—and that he should have taken that more into account when devising the gameplan. But the run had worked all season, and Wilson ended up throwing the ball 27 times, which was exactly the formula that had gotten them that far.

It was a disappointing loss, but the season was a surprise to everyone not in the building at Seahawks headquarters. Many predicted that they would finish below .500, and there were even predictions as low as 4–12. It helped to have two All-Pro players on the team. Bobby Wagner, who could not be a better leader or example of being a professional, had another fantastic year. He could've made the All-Pro team based on his performance in Week 13 against the 49ers alone. He had 12 tackles (two of them for a loss), a quarterback sack, a forced fumble (that he recovered himself for an 11-yard gain), and a spectacular 98-yard interception return for a touchdown. After the game I joked, "Well, I don't know. He could've blocked a kick or something."

The next week against the Vikings, he did just that, blocking a 47-yard field goal with a spectacular leap over the middle of the line. Seven plays later Carson scored a touchdown, putting Minnesota away for good.

The other All-Pro was the rookie punter Michael Dickson, whom the Seahawks had moved up to select out of the University of Texas. Being a crusty old linebacker, it's not like me to gush over punters, but this kid is special. He had a lot of help from three of the best headhunters on any punt team in the NFL. If cornerbacks Neiko Thorpe, Akeem King, and Justin Coleman weren't making spectacular tackles downfield, they were downing punts inside the 10-yard line. Dickson had the best net average in the NFL.

Another star was wide receiver Tyler Lockett, who had his best season as a pro. Lockett had a tough injury at the end of the 2016 season, breaking his leg on a catch he made at the 1-yard line in the penultimate game of the year. Lockett is not your classic outside receiver like Julio Jones or Mike Evans. Those guys are 6'4" and 220 pounds, while Lockett is 5'9" and about 180 on a good day. Yet when it counts, he separates from defensive backs as well as anyone in the league. Just four years into his career, his 6,944 all-purpose yards are No. 40 all time. Since he entered the league in 2015, he is No. 1 in all-purpose yards, leading players like Jones and Todd Gurley. His 57 catches for 965 yards and 10 touchdowns in 2018 are a career best, and he was a huge part of the success the Seahawks had that year.

Dickson was not the only rookie to perform well. Defensive end/ linebacker Jacob Martin, a sixth rounder out of Temple, proved he can be an effective edge rusher. He got better and better and logged three sacks in the final four regular-season games. First-round running back Rashaad Penny got off to a slow start—something rookies tend to do— but finished the season with 85 carries for 419 yards, two touchdowns, and zero fumbles.

Unfortunately, tight end Will Dissly, the fourth-round pick out of University of Washington, injured his knee in Week 4 and spent the majority of the year on injured reserve. It's too bad because he was starting to really get the hang of it. Dissly scored two touchdowns in his first two games and had a 66-yard reception in the opener in Denver. He had been touted as the best blocking tight end in college football and showed that against the Arizona Cardinals, owning defensive end Chandler Jones. His eight catches for 156 yards in just four games proved he can be a complete tight end. Rasheem Green, a defensive end out of USC, and Shaquem Griffin were significant contributors as well. The gem of the draft was Tre Flowers. The safety-turned-corner out of Oklahoma State was as consistent as any player on the defense. I'm always impressed when rookies are able to get up to speed in the NFL. So when a player like Flowers not only starts, but also plays well at a difficult position like cornerback, it bodes well for his future. It seemed to say a lot about where the Seahawks were headed.

CHAPTER 15
THE UNDERRATED

There are some Seahawks players who truly made great contributions and somehow get lost in the record books. After all, you can only put so many players in the Ring of Honor (just nine players as of 2019) and you can only retire so many numbers (four as of 2019). So I wanted to recognize some of the great ones who either didn't get mentioned as much or are underappreciated in Seahawks history.

The original Legion of Boom may be the most underappreciated position group in NFL history. Yes, it does include Kenny Easley, who deservedly made it into the NFL Hall of Fame in 2017 and in the Seahawk Ring of Honor, and a guy like Dave Brown, who is also in the Ring of Honor. But long before the Internet and Twitter were invented, the Seahawks had an unbelievable collection of defensive backs that put up eye-popping numbers in the form of takeaways that rival and even surpass the numbers that the Legion of Boom had.

In 1984 the Seahawks defense had 63 takeaways, which ranks second all time behind the San Diego Chargers, who had 66 takeaways in 1961. Much of that was because of a defensive backfield that was opportunistic to say the least. Besides accomplishing the Herculean task of setting me up with my wife, Paul Moyer was a part of that defense in 1984. His career as a safety for the Seahawks spanned from 1983 to 1989, and the problem for Moyer was he couldn't get on the field because everyone else was so good. When he finally did in 1988, he started all 16 games and had six of his 11 career interceptions as a Seahawks safety. He gushes when he talks about that collection of defensive backs he played with. They were led by defensive backs coach Ralph Hawkins, who was a stickler for details and walk-throughs and practice and route recognition. Moyer calls the following four men the smartest group of football players that he has ever been around.

Dave Brown

Brown tragically passed away six days before his 53rd birthday due to heart failure. More than anything else, he was a person you could count on and was one of the better men I met in the NFL. I went to Brown's funeral in 2006, and based on the number of people in attendance, it was clear what he meant to his teammates and the community.

He was traded my rookie year to the Green Bay Packers and then returned to coach the Seahawks defensive backs in 1992. The Pittsburgh Steelers drafted Brown in the first round out of Michigan, and he won a ring as a member of the Steelers' Super Bowl X champion team. He made it to Seattle because of the expansion draft in 1976 when the Seahawks and the Tampa Bay Buccaneers came into the NFL.

He didn't play much his rookie year in Pittsburgh, but when he got to Seattle, things clicked for him, and he became a turnover machine. During his 11 years in Seattle, he picked off 50 passes, recovered 12 fumbles, and scored five touchdowns. He finished his career in Green Bay and ran his career interception number up to 62, which puts him 10th in NFL history.

Brown was inducted into the Seahawks Ring of Honor in 1992, so it's not that he's that underrated. I'm just not sure he's appreciated as much as he should be for what he did.

Kenny Easley

Easley is also in the Ring of Honor and was recently inducted into the Pro Football Hall of Fame in 2017. He is the fourth player to have that honor who spent his entire career as a Seahawk. So like Dave Brown, he may not be underrated, but I'd argue he's definitely underappreciated for all that he did. He played for only seven years, so you can't help but wonder what kind of numbers Easley could've put up had he lasted as long as Brown. During his short career, he was All-Pro three times and voted into the Pro Bowl five times. Easley was traded in 1988— possibly because he was a vocal leader for the players' union the year before during the strike, or possibly not. Like me after I was traded to the San Francisco 49ers the year before, he failed his physical with the Phoenix Cardinals. He failed his due to signs of kidney failure when he was traded for quarterback Kelly Stouffer. (The Seahawks ended up getting Stouffer anyway.)

It was a shame that Easley couldn't have had a career like Brown's that lasted 15 years, but the way Easley played prohibited that. He was a physical, intimidating safety who threw his body around the field. He was Kam Chancellor 30 years early, or Chancellor was Kenny Easley 30 years later. Interestingly enough, Chancellor grew up in the same area of Virginia as Easley and even briefly dated Easley's daughter. He also watched film of Easley and took great pride in comparisons of their games. Easley was also a playmaker. He scored three touchdowns, intercepted 32 passes, and recovered 11 fumbles.

John Harris

According to Paul Moyer, Harris was the smartest player he ever played with. Moyer would sit next to him on the plane, on the bus rides, and in meetings and try to soak up every bit of knowledge he could absorb. Harris played eight years for the Seahawks as a free safety, and his best year was 1981 when he picked off 10 passes, recovered three fumbles, and scored two touchdowns. He ended his 11-year career with the Minnesota Vikings and, when it was all said and done, he had amassed 50 interceptions, 12 fumble recoveries, and scored two touchdowns.

Keith Simpson

Simpson was a great tackling cornerback, and that was rare in those days. Typically, corners were there to cover and nothing else. But Simpson was in for it all. He was a first-round draft choice out of Memphis State in 1978. Unlike the Legion of Boom, which had one first rounder in Earl Thomas and three late-round draft choices in Richard Sherman, Kam Chancellor, and others, this iteration of the L.O.B. had three first-round draft choices in Kenny Easley, Simpson, and Dave Brown, and one late-rounder in John Harris. Simpson had 19 interceptions in his eight-year career with the Seahawks, picked up seven fumbles, and scored three touchdowns. This opportunistic group worked and studied for everything they got.

In that historic 1984 season, they beat the Kansas City Chiefs 45–0, and Easley, Brown, and Simpson returned four interceptions for touchdowns, including two by Brown for 287 yards in interception returns. It's sort of hard to imagine those Seahawks records will ever be broken. Those players had combined career totals of 163 interceptions, more than 2,100 return yards, 42 fumble recoveries, and 13 touchdowns.

* * *

John L. Williams

Williams was listed as a fullback, but he may have been the most versatile offensive player in Seahawks history. During his eight years with the Seahawks, he rushed for 4,579 yards and amassed 4,151 yards receiving. He scored 33 running and receiving touchdowns. He was 5'11" and 235 pounds. Though he was built like a bowling ball, he had an ability to make tacklers miss and had the softest hands I've ever seen. He had such a smooth transition from catching the ball to running it.

He had dozens of spectacular games, but the best one I remember was in the final game of the 1988 season. We needed to win in order to capture the AFC West title—the first division title in team history—and go to the playoffs, and Williams delivered in a big way. He had 180 yards receiving and 59 yards rushing. In the third quarter, he hauled in a screen pass, which was his specialty, and scored a 75-yard touchdown.

Williams is third on the list of most receptions in Seahawks history with 471 catches, and that's behind only Steve Largent and Brian Blades. He is second on the list (behind Largent) with the most seasons of 50 or more catches, having accomplished that six times.

Williams held out one year, and when he finally reported to camp, it looked like he had just stepped off a bass boat. Physically, he was no Chris Carson. But like Joe Nash, it made what he did on the field

John L. Williams gains some of his 239 total yards in the last game of the 1988 season to help us defeat Los Angeles Raiders and win the AFC West.

that much more impressive. He hit the ground running that year and played as well as anyone in camp. He never missed a beat. That's one of the things that I love about football: good players come in all sizes, shapes, and packages. If you asked me to promote a player into the Ring of Honor, it would probably come down to Nash and Williams.

Keith Butler

Butler is now the defensive coordinator for the Pittsburgh Steelers and has been coaching there as a linebacker coach and defensive coordinator since 2003. But as a player, he was first one of Seattle's great draft choices. The Seahawks selected him in the second round in 1978.

It's no surprise to me that he went on to a long and distinguished coaching career because it was Butts—yep, that's what we called him—who taught me how to play pro football. When I was drafted by Seattle in 1987, Butler came up to me and said in his heavy southern drawl, "Boy, you were drafted here to replace me, so you might as well learn the game." Butts called me "boy" for about two or three months until he thought I had earned my stripes. I stood next to Butts in practices and during games as much as I could. After a lot of plays that I made in the NFL, I would think about Butler and the things he taught me.

When I came to Seattle as a 23-year-old rookie, I looked at Butler and thought I was looking at Father Time. He had a wrist that had been fused, and it couldn't bend backward. He also had his front teeth knocked out at some point and had two silver teeth that looked like he had a bottle cap in his mouth. He had a big reddish/gray beard. To me it looked like he was 80 years old. I thought to myself, *I'm never gonna look like that.* In my ninth and final year in the NFL—outside of the metal front teeth—I looked pretty close to what Butler looked like. Football does that to you.

As good of a mentor and a coach as he was to me, he was just as good as a player. In 2018 Bobby Wagner passed Butler to move into second place in tackles in franchise history. Butler is now third all time with 813 tackles.

Eugene Robinson

"Genie-Rob" is the all-time tackling leader for the Seahawks with 983. His career total is 1,413 with four different teams, which included winning a Super Bowl ring with Mike Holmgren's 1996 Green Bay Packers. That's pretty good for an undrafted player out of Colgate, a small school in New York. We used to tease Robinson that he came from the school that invented toothpaste. There were not—and still aren't—a lot of players in the NFL from Colgate. (In fact, there are only 13 since the merger in 1970, according to Pro Football Reference.) He also had 57 interceptions, including 42 with the Seahawks. He was a lot like Earl Thomas because he played all over the field, even though he was typically lined up deep in his free safety position. As proof of that, consider that he also had 7.5 sacks, 15 forced fumbles, more than 750 interception return yards, and two fumble recoveries.

I was teammates with Robinson my entire time in Seattle, and as good as he was on the field, he was one of my favorite teammates off the field. He was generous with his praise and always made you feel like a million bucks. I've run into Robinson quite often because he also was a longtime color commentator for the Carolina Panthers radio broadcast.

Jon Ryan

The love sent Ryan's way via social media and elsewhere when he was released prior to the 2018 season spoke loudly. How many punters receive that kind of love from an entire fanbase? To be sure, Ryan made a lot of fans with his sense of humor and laid-back off-field attitude, which befits someone who married a comedian named Sarah Colonna.

But for the moment, Ryan has to be considered the best overall punter in Seahawks history due to his consistency and longevity. His pinpoint punting was a big reason the 2013 Super Bowl champion team spent most of the season on the verge of breaking a record for fewest punt return yards allowed before it got away right at the end.

Ryan holds essentially every team punting record. He also threw one of the most famous passes in franchise history—the shotput to tackle Garry Gilliam for a touchdown out of a field-goal formation that sparked the comeback to win the 2015 NFC Championship Game against the Green Bay Packers.

When Seattle moved up to take punter Michael Dickson in the fifth round of the 2018 NFL Draft, you knew that Ryan's days were numbered. But by then he had left an indelible mark in Seahawks history.

Stephen Hauschka

Hauschka deserves mention because it felt like we really didn't talk about him much here in Seattle for quite a while. Again, the kicker shouldn't be talked about. He shouldn't lose you any games. And when he has an opportunity to win a game, he should do so. Maybe that's not fair, but that's sort of how it goes for kickers.

When looking at Hauschka's career in Seattle, all that matters is the 2013 season when the Seahawks won Super Bowl XLVIII and how he performed in the playoffs. He was fantastic. In 2013 he was 33-of-35 or 94 percent with his field goals, including three kicks of more than 50 yards and two overtime game-winners. He was also 44-of-44 on extra points that year, so Pete Carroll rightly began calling him "Hausch Money." Hauschka's playoff record is pretty impeccable as well. He was 27-of-28 in field goals and 19-of-20 on extra points in the postseason.

In the end Hauschka's career with the Seahawks was like offensive line coach Tom Cable's career. It worked until—for some odd reason—it stopped working. The 2016 season got a little rough, as he missed a few kicks that could have won games against the Arizona Cardinals that the Seahawks either tied or lost. He also was getting expensive to keep around. But he was a big part of that Super Bowl victory and numerous other big wins along the way, and to me that's what stands out the most.

Bobby Engram

In Engram's eight years with the Seahawks, he had 18 touchdowns and 4,859 yards receiving. And to this day, Engram holds the team's single-season reception record with 94 catches in 2007. That 2007 season was Engram's best. He had 1,147 yards, six touchdowns, and a catch-to-target rate of 70 percent.

Engram's specialties were third-down receptions and precise route running—much like Doug Baldwin, who tied Engram's single-season record in 2016. Engram was Matt Hasselbeck's go-to guy on third down because Hasselbeck and Engram were always on the same page—sort of the same way Baldwin has been in recent years with Russell Wilson.

At Penn State, Engram won the Biletnikoff Trophy as the nation's best college receiver. For the past eight years, he's been coaching wide receivers in the NFL with the San Francisco 49ers and Pittsburgh Steelers and is currently the tight ends coach with the Baltimore Ravens. He was the kind of route runner and football player that would make a great coach.

Darrell Jackson

D-Jack was also a player who was on the same page as Matt Hasselbeck. After a game in 2005, Hasselbeck told us one of the touchdown passes to Jackson was created by non-verbal communication. The defense gave the same look in a similar situation, and Hasselbeck just nodded at Jackson and put it up for the receiver, who was wide open for a touchdown.

Jackson shows up in the Seahawks record books quite often, and Doug Baldwin surpassed him in all-time yardage in 2018. As a Seahawks receiver, Jackson has 6,445 yards, putting him fourth in team history. He's also second in games with 100 or more yards (19) and one of the few Seahawks with 80 or more catches in a single season.

Joey Galloway

Galloway played in the NFL until 2010, spending his last 11 seasons with teams other than the Seahawks. But the numbers show he was one of the most productive players in team history, and during some of the desultory years in the changeover from Ken Behring to Paul Allen, he often was one of the only things to get excited about.

In just five years with Seattle, Galloway remains sixth in team history in receiving yards with 4,457 and fourth in touchdowns with 37. His 12 touchdowns in 1997 are tied for third most in a season in team history. He has the Seahawks record for the most reception yardage for a rookie with 1,039 yards in 1995. He's 36th in NFL history in receiving yards with 10,950. Galloway also was a really good returner—as evidenced by his four punt returns for touchdowns, which is the most in team history. No one else has more than two. Galloway was sort of what Pete Carroll and John Schneider hoped Percy Harvin could be. He also had 45 rushing attempts for 378 yards in his Seattle career and a long of 86.

Ricky Watters

Many NFL fans associate Watters with the San Francisco 49ers and Philadelphia Eagles. But while he played just the final four years of his career with the Seahawks, Watters left quite a legacy. Watters is sixth in team history with 4,009 yards from those four seasons, which occurred during a pretty turbulent time for the franchise.

After winning a ring with the 49ers and playing with the Eagles, he signed with the Seahawks during the last year of Dennis Erickson's regime. He then endured the changeover to Mike Holmgren and playing at Husky Stadium. I always thought he played his butt off, even though he had to sort of wonder what the heck he'd gotten himself into. He started every game from 1998 to 2000, getting 319, 325, and 278 carries, gaining 1,239, 1,210, and 1,242 yards in those years, respectively, and 4.5 yards per carry in 2000. And he also had 52, 40, and 63 receptions in those years. He broke a bone in his ankle in 2001 and played only five games and never played again. I think people simply forget how productive he was in those years.

Shawn Springs

For many people, Springs' Seahawks legacy is hard to separate from the high expectations that greeted his arrival during the 1997 NFL Draft. The Seahawks actually took Springs third overall that day and waited until three picks later to select Walter Jones, who went on to be one of the best ever at his position of left tackle.

But Springs started 88 games over seven years and made the Pro Bowl in his second season in 1998 when he had seven interceptions, returning two for touchdowns. He also returned a fumble for a touchdown that season, ranking fifth on the team in scoring. Each of his scores came in games the Seahawks won during an 8–8 season, in which they almost made the playoffs. If nothing else, scoring three touchdowns is one of the more unusual feats for a defensive player in team history. He scored four overall in his Seattle career. The only defensive player with more is Dave Brown with five. Springs is also tied for eighth in team history in interceptions with 20, which is one behind Marcus Trufant.

Chris Warren

Warren had the misfortune of playing for the Seahawks during the end of the Chuck Knox era and then into the Tom Flores/Ken Behring mid-1990s doldrums. So a lot of fans may not remember him, but in eight years with the Seahawks, Warren ran for more than 6,700 yards and 44 touchdowns. He was named to three Pro Bowls and surpassed 1,000 yards four times.

Warren came to Seattle in a great 1990 draft out of tiny Ferrum College as a fourth rounder. That draft included Cortez Kennedy and linebacker Terry Wooden and is arguably as good as any in team history.

(Too bad the Seahawks just didn't have a few more to stave off some of the bad times that were to come.)

He was a bruising ball carrier with an upright style of running and he would run through you if necessary. He had a ridiculous 40-yard dash time for a guy who was 6'2" and 230 pounds. Like a lot of players in that era, it's just too bad the franchise was in such chaos and they won so few games.

Marcus Trufant

Tru was part of a good Seahawks defense in an era when most people thought of the Seahawks for their offense. But his play helped the Seahawks win the NFC West four years in a row under Mike Holmgren. His 21 career interceptions are seventh in team history on a team with a lot of great defensive backs in their past. Trufant was the consummate Washington man. He lettered and excelled in football, track, and basketball at Wilson High School in Tacoma and received a scholarship to Washington State. He might well have gone to UW, as did his younger brother Desmond, but—in what was one of their bigger recruiting misses—the Huskies didn't offer him at the time. After helping lead the Cougars to a Pac-10 title and a Rose Bowl berth (beating Pete Carroll's USC team in 2002 to do so), Trufant became the 11th overall pick in the 2003 draft and he spent his entire 10-year career (other than a few days in camp with the Jacksonville Jaguars) in Seattle.

At 5'11" and just under 200 pounds, Trufant was more than willing to hit. He had 644 tackles and was a technician who took pride in his ability to tackle. One of the more difficult things for defensive backs is to handle the straight-arm from opposing ball carriers. Defenders' hands are usually down, and they lead with their facemask, making them extremely vulnerable to the straight-arm. If it's executed properly, it can be devastating. Trufant had a way of anticipating the straight-arm and did a great job of chopping or hacking it down and making the tackle.

Trufant's best year was 2007 when he had seven interceptions, one of them for a touchdown, and an appearance in the Pro Bowl. His last year in Seattle was 2012, and he did a great job of mentoring the Legion of Boom. It's sort of too bad he couldn't hang around for that season and get a ring. A cornerback who can both cover and tackle is rare, and Trufant was a gem.

Jordan Babineaux

Big Play Babs was one of the great undrafted free agents in NFL history. His final stat line was more than 600 tackles, eight forced fumbles, four fumble recoveries, 12 interceptions, and three defensive touchdowns. Those stats alone put him as one of the great Seahawks of all time. But it was more about the timing of the plays that he made.

Amongst his well-timed plays, he forced a fumble on a punt return in 2005 against the St. Louis Rams that keyed the win that began their 11-game winning streak. Two weeks later against the Dallas Cowboys, he picked off Drew Bledsoe and returned it 25 yards with 14 seconds on the clock. Kicker Josh Brown then kicked a game-winning, 50-yard field goal to give the Seahawks a 13–10 win. In 2007 he returned an interception 57 yards for a touchdown to ice a playoff win against the Washington Redskins.

What was probably his most memorable play came during a divisional playoff game against the Cowboys after the 2006 season. The Seahawks were nursing a 21–20 lead, and with 1:13 left in the fourth quarter, the Cowboys lined up for what would be the game-winning field goal on fourth and 1 at the Seattle 2-yard line. Quarterback Tony Romo, who was the holder, bobbled the snap and took off for the goal line. Just when it looked like he would get the first down and possibly score the game-winning touchdown, Babineaux tracked down Romo from behind, tackling him for no gain, and putting the Seahawks in the second round of the playoffs. It was one of the greatest, most adrenaline-filled plays in Seahawks history. Plays like that are what Babineaux was all about.

Jeff "Boogie" Bryant

I had the pleasure of playing my entire career in Seattle behind Bryant. He was a great teammate and always had your back on and off the field. Like Jacob Green and Joe Nash, Bryant was unselfish and, if he couldn't make a play, he would make sure that one of his teammates could. He was listed at 6'5" and 275 pounds, but in full pads, he was a giant and he played bigger than his actual size.

I can't believe he isn't talked about more in Seahawks history. He was a first-round pick (No. 6 overall) in the 1982 draft out of Clemson and played his entire 12-year career in Seattle. His 63 sacks are third in Seahawks history. In 1984 he recorded 14.5 sacks and was a big part of that historically good playmaking defense that took the ball away 63 times. It was a crime that he was never selected to the Pro Bowl.

Brian Blades

Until Doug Baldwin came around, Blades was undoubtedly the second best receiver in Seahawks history. (He may now have to share that title.) Blades was small and quick but also tough as hell. It seemed like he caught everything.

Blades was listed at 5'11" and 189 pounds, and I think that was being generous. But that didn't stop him from going across the middle and taking big shots from defenders like Ronnie Lott. He was instrumental in helping us win the division in 1988. As a rookie that season, he caught 40 passes for 682 yards and eight touchdowns and had a 17.1 yard-per-catch average. In the Seahawks record books, Blades is everywhere. He ranks No. 2 in catches with 581, first in most seasons with 80 or more catches in a season, and is third in most consecutive games with a catch at 52.

Curt Warner

C-Dubs left Penn State as the third pick of the 1983 draft behind John Elway and Eric Dickerson, and the Seahawks moved up to get him in what was the first big move of the Chuck Knox era. And it was Warner who truly added the Ground to Ground Chuck during those 1980s glory days at the Kingdome. Warner owned 42 school records at that time and was the all-time leading rusher up until 2010. His 18 100-yard rushing games is still a Penn State record.

As a Seahawks player, he knew how to make an entrance. On his first carry of his rookie year—Opening Day against the Kansas City Chiefs—he ran for a 60-yard gain, and fans have said that was one of the loudest spontaneous cheers they remember from the old Kingdome.

He finished that season with 1,449 yards and 13 touchdowns. He was poised to take off in his second year before suffering an ACL injury in the first game of the season.

Some have said that maybe Warner was never the same, but his hard work to rehabilitate that injury paid off. He ran for more than 1,000 yards in three of the next four seasons and might have made it four out of five if not for the strike-shortened 1987 season, when he just missed the 1,000-yard mark with 985 yards. He ran for more than 1,000 in four of his six seasons with the Seahawks and was a three-time Pro Bowler.

Warner was always one of my favorite teammates, though it didn't start out that way. In my first mini-camp just after the 1987 draft, I had to cover him man-to-man. He beat me with an out-and-up move, and I grabbed his jersey and jabbed him right in the neck with my thumb. I remember thinking, *Oh man, I just fouled Curt Warner! I'm off to a bad start!* I think he mumbled something about me being a stupid rookie, but he was right. He was funny, a great leader, and had a lot of grit, as evidenced by his battling back from that devastating knee injury.

He and his wife, Anna Warner, are amazing parents to Austin and Christian, their twins with autism, and have two other children, Jonathan and Isabella. He detailed their family's journey in a book he co-wrote called *The Warner Boys: Our Family's Story of Autism and Hope.*

Michael Sinclair

My last year in Seattle, Sinclair was a rookie, and there was never a better example of the saying: rookies are meant to be seen and not heard. Sinclair was so quiet you hardly knew he was there. However, in the years after I left, he was heard in a big way. To this day he still has the single-season sack record for the Seahawks; he recorded 16.5 in 1998. He is second behind Jacob Green in career sacks with 73.5 and second in forced fumbles with 25. Being second to Green is an honor; Sinclair was a three-time Pro Bowler from 1996 to 1998 and in those three years alone recorded 41.5 sacks. Sinclair has more sacks than anyone in the 1991 draft, which is significant, considering he was drafted in the sixth round out of Eastern New Mexico.

Sherman Smith

Smith was the first offensive player picked by the new expansion team called the Seattle Seahawks. The second rounder out of University of Miami (Ohio) was also the first Seahawks back to rush for more than 100 yards. He ran for 124 yards in a game against the Atlanta Falcons, which represented the first time the Seahawks beat a non-expansion team. He was the team's leading rusher in the first four years of the Seahawks existence, and by the end of his career in Seattle, his receiving and running totals were 5,771 yards and 38 touchdowns.

He then went into coaching, starting his career at Redmond High School on the east side of Seattle, and went on to coach for his alma mater at Miami. In the professional ranks, he coached for the Houston Oilers/Tennessee Titans franchise, was the offensive coordinator for the Washington Redskins for two years, and coached running backs in Seattle for nine years during the championship era of Seahawks football.

In 2017 ESPN's Sarah Spain wrote an amazing story involving Smith and Kansas City Chiefs running back coach Deland McCullough that not even Hollywood could have scripted. McCullough was adopted at a very young age and never knew who his birth parents were. Growing up in Youngstown, Ohio, he always felt restless, not knowing his true identity. He took his frustration out on the football field and was soon on a lot of college football recruiting lists as a high school football player.

One of those schools was Miami (Ohio), where Smith was coaching running backs. McCullough was a running back. For the first time in his life, he felt that the football coaches who came to recruit him, like Smith, were true male role models. So he followed Smith to Miami, where he had a spectacular career. After a failed attempt to make it in the NFL because of injury, he followed Smith's career path coaching football. The two always stayed in touch, and while McCullough was coaching at USC, he accepted an offer from Smith to do a coaching internship in 2016 with the Seattle Seahawks. The two were inseparable. The coaches and players in Seattle would often tease them because they were always together, and they walked the same and talked the same.

The now 44-year-old McCullough had started a family of his own, and it always bothered him that every time he filled out a birth certificate for his own four children he didn't have his birth parents' information. Meanwhile, laws changed in Ohio and Pennsylvania in 2016, enabling adoption records to be unsealed that were previously held under lock and key. Finally, McCullough was able to research his past. He contacted who he thought was his birth mother through Facebook.

Once they talked on the phone, McCullough and his birth mother, Carol Briggs, hit it off immediately, and both were entirely convinced that they were indeed related. Eventually, McCullough came around to the question that was hanging in the air: "Who is my father?" She answered that it was "a man named Sherman Smith." When McCullough was told who his father was, his knees buckled and he had to lean against a wall to keep himself upright. His response to Briggs was: "I've known Sherman my whole life."

In 1972 Smith had a brief fling with Briggs before he went off to college. When she found out she was pregnant at age 16, Briggs and her parents decided to keep it a secret and give the baby up for adoption.

Her parents sent her off to have the baby and turn him over to the state at Zoar Home for Mothers, Babies, and Convalescents. Only Briggs, her parents, and her aunt knew about the existence of McCullough, whose birth certificate name was Jon Kenneth Briggs, until 44 years later. Smith had a similar reaction when McCullough called him with that news. Smith was 62 years old and had his own family. He had been married to his college sweetheart for 42 years with two grown children and had not thought about Briggs for decades. At first, Smith told McCullough that he needed a few moments to process all of this. You can understand why. But when they were reunited for the first time after that, Smith embraced McCullough and said two words: "My son."

McCullough and Smith are both in the Miami (Ohio) Athletic Hall of Fame. Smith has mentored a lot of young men in his amazing life and is one of those people you wish there were more of. It's an amazing love story, and their relationship has continued on in a much more special way—as father and son.

CHAPTER 16
SEA GALS AND SEAHAWKS

I'm not sure if football players and cheerleaders always go together. It seems like a cliché, right? But they sure seemed to go together in Seattle. My linebacker coach Rusty Tillman married a Seahawks cheerleader. My friend and teammate, Paul Moyer, a safety, married a Seahawks cheerleader. I married a Seahawks cheerleader, Shannen, and have been married for 26 years.

You often hear that cheerleaders are forbidden from dating the players, but I'm not sure if it really is a policy across the NFL or just a rumor. Back in my day, it was supposedly an unspoken agreement, but today cheerleading is pretty big business, and there are groups, like the Dallas Cowboys cheerleaders, who have to sign an agreement that they will not fraternize with the Cowboys players. Shannen and Heather, Paul's wife, used to get two tickets to home games and they made a little bit of money doing appearances around town during the week. In the mid-1980s, a few Sea Gals took a promotional trip to Juneau, Alaska, where there are a lot of dedicated Seahawks fans who were starved for Seahawks live appearances. Shannen told me the appearance was at a mall, and the line for autographs went outside and around the corner of the mall. Today there are Pro Bowl cheerleaders, and they get free hair, makeup, and clothing allowances. Shannen and I jokingly complain about the fact that guys with my talent make more in one season than I did in my entire nine-year career and that today's Sea Gals get much more than two free tickets for home games. But it's all in fun. We both love the fact that we had the opportunity to play (and cheer) in that era of Seahawks football.

So to guys like Tillman, Moyer, and myself, those agreements sound ridiculous. Why would some hokey, made-up regulation keep two people apart? Well, it didn't in Seattle. I'm sure that Moyer and Tillman were much smoother than I was, though. When I first came to Seattle in 1987, I saw the cheerleaders out at practice in Kirkland, Washington, at our training facility and first laid eyes on Shannen. I thought, *Who is that?* I thought my wife—then fantasy girl—was the most beautiful girl I had ever seen who wasn't on TV or in a magazine. But it would be years before I mustered up the courage to ask her out. Well, actually, I didn't even do that.

e playing linebacker for the Seahawks from 1987 to 1992, I also met my future wife, Shannen, a Sea Gals
rleader.

There were a couple of failed attempts at being smooth. Turns out I was a player, not a playa. Three years later in 1990, we were both doing an autograph signing appearance at a local car dealership. I tried to strike up conversation with her, but I was just not one for small talk. I tried to ask her questions about being a cheerleader and whatnot. For some reason at one point, out of my mouth came: "So when you guys cheer, do you get sweaty?" *Idiot!* I was horrified by what had just come out of my mouth. Like I said, *real smooth.*

I ran into her a few more times in the years that followed, but we were both dating others, and it just never worked out, even though we ran in the same circles. But mercifully, my buddy and teammate Moyer—whose wife, Heather, was Shannen's friend—was standing next to me during a Monday practice, and we started talking about an event that night at a local bar that would have both players and Sea Gals in attendance. I was trying to pay attention to practice, but when Moyer said, "A certain blonde cheerleader is asking if you'll be there tonight," I lost all interest in practice. I must've repeated to Moyer four times: "Are you messing with me? "Are you serious?" "If this is a joke, we're not friends anymore!" So I never really asked her out. It was the equivalent of someone passing me a note in study hall. I imagined a note, saying: "Do you like Shannen?" with a box to check "yes" or "no."

After a few bottles of liquid courage later that night at the bar, my big move was to hook my feet under her chair and scoot her over next to me. I thought she was dating sophisticated, billionaire European male models. But she liked that I wasn't smooth. I was more like an ordinary guy because I drove a Ford Bronco instead of a fancy sports car, had a dog named Lefty, and liked to stay home and watch movies rather than go out all the time. So to my fellow dorks out there who have no game, there is hope for you.

To this day Moyer likes to say, "Actually, I'm responsible for your kids." I'm not sure I am comfortable with that phrasing, but I am grateful to him and Heather for helping get us together. We are still great friends and see each other all the time. When Moyer takes too much credit, I tell him, "Moyer, you and I are old friends. That means that I know everything about you, and I like you anyway."

I often think about what would've happened if I had not been drafted by the Seahawks. When I first met Seahawks defensive back coach and future head coach Jim Mora in 2007, the question of fate became even more surreal to me. Before I was drafted in 1987, the then-San Diego Chargers were thinking about selecting me. I had even talked to their general manager Bobby Beathard before the draft, but once the Seahawks picked me, I never gave it a second thought. Then I met Mora.

Mora was one of the NFL's first quality control coaches, a position he served for the Chargers in 1987. It was a post that became popular for young coaches to start out at while beginning their coaching careers. When I introduced myself to Mora, he said, "You were one of the biggest draft day arguments I have ever seen." He went on to tell me that the head coach, Al Saunders, who had recruited me out of high school at Cal, wanted to choose me with their first-round pick while Beathard wanted to draft a running back named Rod Bernstine out of Texas A&M. As Mora explained the situation to me, he started getting more and more animated. He said: "Then the draft clock started ticking down, and they were still fighting about it. The clock was at 10...9...8, and they were still fighting. I thought time was going to expire, and we would lose the pick! Finally, the owner [Dean Spanos] stepped in and said, 'Just take Bernstine.'"

My head started spinning. I was born in San Diego, and surely my entire family would've ended up back there. I would've had a different career and had a different wife and different kids for crying out loud. All that I have—my whole world—was because the Seahawks drafted me in the second round. Every year I think about the young men coming out in the draft and how their futures, including who they marry and their eventual families, may hang in the balance as my fate did, and it's all based on what a bunch of coaches and scouts think about their ability to play football.

CHAPTER 17
PAUL ALLEN AND OTHER FINAL REFLECTIONS

When the Seahawks came home from London with a win against the Oakland Raiders in the middle of October 2018, it was to sad news. Their owner, Mr. Paul Allen, had passed away from cancer. First diagnosed with Hodgkin's lymphoma when he was just 29, he was diagnosed with non-Hodgkin's lymphoma in 2009. After undergoing treatment for it, the disease reoccurred in 2018. Allen co-founded Microsoft with Bill Gates in 1975 and then became an investor and one of the great philanthropists in American history. He was also a fantastic owner. He had owned the Portland Trail Blazers of the NBA since 1988 and then became the owner and savior of the Seattle Seahawks in 1996 when Ken Behring tried to move the Seahawks to Los Angeles.

Allen was the ultimate Seattlite. Born and raised in Seattle, he attended Washington State University for a while before heading to Boston where he co-founded Microsoft. But he eventually returned to Seattle. He not only saved the Seahawks from leaving town, but also made huge investments that will make a lasting legacy all over the city, such as the Museum of Pop Culture in Seattle and the Flying Heritage & Combat Armor Museum.

He was known as a reclusive, private person, and it was rare to see him around Seahawks headquarters. What he did best as an owner was to hire the right people. He brought in Mike Holmgren, Pete Carroll, and John Schneider and presided over two great eras in Seahawks history.

His sister, Jody, took over for the remainder of the 2018 season, and though there was talk about who would be the next owner, for now the team is staying in the hands of the Paul G. Allen Trust with Jody as the chairman, securing the immediate future of a team that Paul Allen long ago secured for Seattle. Jody's first move was to extend Carroll's contract, ensuring that Carroll and Schneider will be together through the 2021 season. I don't think there is a better coach/general manager combo in the league. Schneider has a way of finding those players—like Richard Sherman, Kam Chancellor, K.J. Wright, and Doug Baldwin— particularly in the later rounds of the draft and free agency, and Carroll has a way of identifying exactly what he's looking for at each position, especially on defense.

Maybe the most disappointing outcome of Super Bowl XLIX is that it perhaps made the case for Carroll's enshrinement in the NFL Hall of Fame less strong. But even if that's the case, there is still time. With Bobby Wagner and Russell Wilson in place, he has two of the best leaders on either side of the ball in the NFL, and with the ability to draft and develop players, there is hope that the Seahawks can get back to the Super Bowl in the near future.

Even without another Super Bowl title, I believe there's enough to get Carroll into the Hall of Fame with the run he had from 2012 through 2016. He oversaw a historically good defense that led the NFL in scoring defense four years in a row and five straight years of double-digit wins, five straight trips to the playoffs, two conference championships, and one world championship.

He's also the oldest coach in the league with the youngest attitude. He's not what you would call old school, but he does have his limits. His No. 1 rule for the team, and I think it's a faultless rule is: protect the team. His players love him because he's open to their causes and concerns. He's also not as stodgy as I am regarding the new rules about helmet-to-helmet hits and some of the safety issues. He's from an old-school era, but his ability to adapt is amazing. He accepts things as they are and moves on with the new reality as well as any person I've ever met. I've learned a lot from Carroll and wish I had the opportunity to play for him.

Carroll has the benefit of getting to coach Wilson, who I cannot envision in anything other than a Seahawks uniform. I see him playing here for at least 15 years. He's the healthiest quarterback—if not the healthiest player in the NFL. And if he truly plays 15 or more years, then I think you are looking at a certain Hall of Famer.

Analysts and those in the media, like myself, have tried to pigeonhole Wilson. Some have said he's benefited from great defenses. The reality is that he's played well with great defenses and played well with middle-of-the-road defenses. Wilson led the league in touchdown passes in 2017 and was third in touchdowns and quarterback rating in 2018. The Seahawks defense ranked 11th and 16th in yards per game in 2017 and 2018.

Some have said he's a good quarterback only when he's on the run. There is no doubt he is good outside of the pocket, but he has proven that he can be a pure pocket passer as well, including when he was a 73 percent passer while throwing 31 touchdowns and just seven interceptions while passing from the pocket in 2015.

Some have said he's just the beneficiary of a great run game. Sure, that part is true. But you could say that for any quarterback, and the year when Wilson had his worst running game was in 2017 when only one other player, J.D. McKissic, scored a rushing touchdown. Wilson ran for three touchdowns and threw 34 touchdowns—more than anyone in the league that year, including Tom Brady and Drew Brees. Wilson can thrive in any offense and in any NFL city because he's so competitive and so dedicated to his craft. But again, I don't see any reason for him to leave nor any reason the Seahawks would part ways with him.

Though Earl Thomas and Sherman went out on a negative note, I think they will be welcomed back with open arms by Seahawks fans five to 10 years from now when it's time to celebrate those Super Bowl teams and the Legion of Boom. We all remember that Brett Favre left the Green Bay Packers for the New York Jets and the hated (in Green Bay) Minnesota Vikings at the end of his career. But it didn't take too long until he was back at Lambeau Field with Bart Starr and being honored by a full house of Packers fans, who were grateful for what he did for the Pack.

I loved those guys for who they were as people as well. Sherman was in your face and unapologetically going to let you hear about everything he did. At a time when Seattle was sort of thought as South Alaska, he helped put us back on the map. Chancellor was shy and soft-spoken, but as Chuck Knox used to say, "I'm gonna speak softly, so you can listen real hard." When he spoke, everyone listened. Thomas was a wild-card. You never knew what he was going to say. And when he said things, you sometimes didn't know what he meant. But he was a wild man on gameday and threw himself all over the field.

When it was all said and done, Chancellor ended up a four-time Pro Bowler and recorded 640 tackles, 12 interceptions, nine forced fumbles, an amazing 17 tackles for a loss (those are hard to get for players in the secondary), and a safety. On top of that, in the postseason he had 97 tackles, three interceptions, and a (team playoff record) 90-yard interception return for a touchdown. Thomas was a three-time All-Pro, a six-time Pro Bowler, and had 684 tackles, 28 interceptions, 11 tackles for loss (also amazing for a safety), and two touchdowns. His playoff numbers were 82 tackles, nine passes defensed, and two interceptions. Sherman had more than 400 tackles, 32 interceptions, five forced fumbles, and two touchdowns. In the postseason he had 42 tackles, two interceptions, and 10 passes defensed. I have made the case on my radio show that he is the best tackling cornerback in NFL history. He's aggressive and takes pride in it, which is rare for a cornerback.

You'll see that these numbers don't quite live up to the numbers of the players from the mid-1980s. Not to take anything away from Dave Brown, Kenny Easley, and John Harris, but quarterbacks have gotten so much better at taking care of the ball. In the 1980s you often saw top 10 quarterbacks with more interceptions than touchdowns. Now quarterbacks like Wilson put up more than 30 touchdowns and just 10 or 11 interceptions. It is also much more difficult playing defense with the penalties and expanded pass interference calls. I can't imagine how Easley would've reacted to getting a penalty like Chancellor did when he separated San Francisco 49ers tight end Vernon Davis from the ball on the 2-yard line in 2012. Hopefully, this current group of Shaquill Griffin, Tre Flowers, Tedric Thompson, Delano Hill, and Bradley McDougald will become the next version of great Seahawks defensive backs to make a name for themselves in the Pacific Northwest.

Everybody knows the adage that in great organizations or companies, success comes from the top down. The Seahawks have been fortunate to have two of the greatest owners in the history of the NFL. The first was John Nordstrom, who is still involved with the team and took a chance in 1976 by starting a great franchise and hiring the right people like general manager Mike McCormick and coaches Jack Patera and Knox.

"Mr. John" is on a lot of the road trips, on the sidelines at practice and the home games, and he's one of my favorite people to talk to. The second was the late Allen, who saved the team by getting a stadium built and hiring Holmgren, Carroll, and Schneider to put a competitive product on the field almost every single year.

I'm in my 24th year as a player and broadcaster for the Seahawks and I have encountered some great people along the way. Some of those people are Gary Wright; Sandy Gregory; Dave Pearson, who was a media intern when I played and is now a vice president; Paul Johns; Julie Barber; Chuck Arnold; and the late Jim Whitesel, who was a trainer that always took good care of his players.

Another is Sam Adkins, a former quarterback for the Seahawks who has a rare distinction. He was not only the last player to wear the No. 12 jersey—now retired for the 12th Man—but he also served as a broadcaster on radio and television, and his construction company repaired and helped build both of the Seahawks facilities. His roommate when he played, the great Steve Raible, is my radio partner in the booth and was a second-round draft choice for the Seahawks like me. Because of those great people and every player mentioned in this book, it has been a thrill to watch this franchise become a multi-billion dollar business and one of the best sports franchises in the world. I plan to stay involved and keep watching for many more years to come. With the Seahawks you know there will be lots of interesting stories to tell.

ACKNOWLEDGMENTS

I would like to thank, first and foremost, my wife, Shannen, for putting up with me burying myself in my computer to write this book. My children, Jake and Kendall, for telling me when something was "boring and sucks!"

I'd also like to thank all of my coaches and teammates for making for a great life. Football is my life, and the relationships that have come along with it have made my life what it is. People in Seattle like Rusty Tillman, Chuck Knox, Tom Catlin, Gary Wright, and John Nordstrom. To all the great high school coaches out there, like my coach Joe Sellers, local coaches like Ed Lucero, Tom Bainter, and John Eagle, and the great college coaches I had like Jack Elway, Paul Wiggin, Dick Manini, and Larry Kerr. You guys are where it all starts for guys like me.

I also want to thank Pete Carroll and my good friend John Schneider, who have made football great again in Seattle. What a ride!

Lastly, ProFootballReference.com, Seattle Seahawks media guides and record books, and the archives of *The Seattle Times* served as valuable resources for Bob and I during the writing of this book.